INTRODUCTION

Herein lie the thoughts of a converted Christian, fresh from years of the wild and wiles of nonsense. Borne from ancient standards of a long past age that sought meaning to our inner life, this small volume presents the ideas we need to carry us upwards and inwards from the common stock of beliefs.

***

The following pages are taken from a number of reflections or homilies given during the years of 2011 to 2015, at St. Phillips in the Hills Episcopal Church in Tucson, Arizona. They were all delivered during the Sunday afternoon ceremony at the 'Come and See' service, a more relaxed and communal circle of friends than the usual and larger morning gatherings.

As a result, the talks ranged over a broader spectrum of spiritual topics, some which are new cast from old subjects, some from material thought passé to a modern understanding of Christianity, and finally, some concepts from the rich literature that thrived just before or after the life of Jesus.

They are all fossils come alive and constitute the signal and sign for Christianity and God at the deepest philosophical and practical level.

CONTENTS

Title   **Page**

WHY AM I CHRISTIAN

3 April 2011

In 1961 I read a little book called, "Why I Am Not A Christian" by Bertrand Russell, a famous philosopher from Wales. It was just what I needed at the time to spring away from my suffocating Catholic schooling.

He was an avowed atheist and his idea that religion was a disease born from fear and a source of untold miseries was raw meat for my grinder. A reviewer said that Russell attacked religion with a stone cold logic.

I took his arguments and ran with them, but not very far. I ran out of gas as soon as I started thinking for myself. For some reason, the idea of religion and all the attendant issues seemed important to me. I decided to give myself 50 years to ruminate & cogitate on these things. Well, my 50 years are up now, but I just put in for an extension.

*

So, here is my preliminary report, 50 years in the making:

First, regarding Bertrand Russell, logic, even 'stone cold logic,' gets lost in a maze trying to comprehend human concerns. Life, as it turns out, is too unstable to use as a placeholder for mathematical certainty. He sputters in the face of emotion as a motive for religion.

Actually, to see life with any wisdom, intellect <u>and</u> emotion has to be in balance. Each has its own intelligence and contribution. We have two eyes and two ears so we can have depth perception. The same goes for thinking and feeling. Too much of one skews the worldview. Logic and reason, without the counterweight of warmth and passion, can turn human affairs cold and lifeless.

Russell's logic isolates and promotes incidents that prove some lopsided attitude and dismisses the many things that put it in doubt. For instance, Russell bolstered his claims with old news of the Inquisition and violence during the Reformation. But he conveniently left out the countless non-religious slaughters that darken our history, from Cain to Laughner. The three barbarians, Stalin, Mao, and Hitler massacred something over 100 million out of shear meanness, not religious fervor.

Alas, the cause of our miseries of this sort are not the fault of a religion, they are the responsibility of the male gender. They are the primary instigators of most overt violent acts against humanity. To foist blame on a religion is the old trick of misdirection. It was men who invented the battle-ax, the thumb-screw, and the atom bomb. Men flail at each other under whatever flag or creed is convenient.

Further, Russell and the people of his ilk, never consider the unseen world, which Christ was speaking to and about. The Gospels are full of stories that can only be understood allegorically. Russell derides them with a literal interpretation. The Bible wouldn't open up to him and reveal its secrets, so he had only the words and not the meaning to work with.

Rereading his book while I was preparing this talk I found Bertrand Russell superficial and mean spirited. He sure changed in all those years.

He calls Jesus cruel for killing that poor unproductive fig tree and sending those demons into those innocent pigs. He failed to grasp the lessons tied to such spiritual stories.

In fact, if I may diverge here for a moment, it is stories that link people in common bond. We all have stories in us that we believe and from which we operate. Genesis and most of the first five books of the Old Testament were not true accounts, but allegories about the condition of man. The first story about a man and woman who had everything, but wanted more, did not happen then, but it happens everyday.

7

The second story about the jealousy and murder of one man by another did not happen then, but also happens everyday. The great story of Moses and the trials of the early Hebrews may not have happened in fact, but it forged the most remarkable people in history. These are not myths, which are fantasy and lack lessons, but metaphors in story form that pack a wallop.

Stories do not have to be true, but if a story has the ring of Truth it reverberates to the human heart and excites the imagination, sweeping time and distance aside. If I tell you a story that moves you, as I like to do since I am a storyteller, it is because of the element of Truth and not the facts. Truth can only be realized, not reasoned.

Stories are the first and best of arts, the spur that gives us motive for social intercourse. Without stories we could not have religion. They are lights that help us see in the dark. Some people sneer at our stories of old, snorting their gall at our naïveté. But they do not have the ears to hear. They need to be heard from inside, not outside.

Without a doubt, the ear is more powerful than the eye. What we hear and carry forward is the call to action. Even reading requires that we speak the words silently to ourselves so we can hear them. Plus, we talk to ourselves constantly so we can hear what we are thinking. In that, sight is subservient to sound because only by sound can we receive our life-giving stories.

*

Christianity spread so rapidly throughout the world 2000 years ago because of its story. No more beautiful and accessible religion had ever been presented to mankind. Without restriction, it was offered to all individuals, classes and nations.   Poverty was no barrier. Neither was ill health or past behavior. It opened itself to the miserable and maimed, the haughty and high. It offered a new dignity and compassion not yet seen on earth. Its revealed doctrine promised forgiveness to men and women imprisoned in their base passions. It brought a new vitality to brotherhood, kindness, decency and peace. In the early days it offered hope to a world bereft of promise. It conquered the Western world because there was need finally for goodness and optimism. The pagan world offered no such respite, being devoid of hopeful stories.

Because it was later twisted and perverted for nefarious purposes should bring no disrepute on the golden opportunity it represents. At its core, and what can still be discovered under the folds of costume and ceremony, is a purity and piety that is still desperately needed in our wild and wicked world. Jesus was a humble carpenter who built a bridge out of a cross. He only asks that we walk that bridge.

So, I am a Christian because I made a discovery quite on my own. I found a pearl of great price and am hanging on to it for dear life. Where Bertrand Russell found only hard, rocky soil, I found plowed ground to grow in. Where he saw vineyards and kings and swine, I saw Faith, Hope, and Love.

In retrospect, the suffocating Catholic schooling does not seem so bad now. It was a good education and luckily they had priests and nuns who gave me a taste of theology that I am now able to digest.

Two of my teachers from that era, Fr. Roy and Fr. Florian died a few years ago. They were the ones, more than any, whose words poured out <u>then</u> that stir me today. I can still hear the echoes of that teaching now. "Heaven is not a place of flutes and lutes, wings and haloes. Heaven is Goodness and only the good can find it." So, for Goodness sake, and for Heaven's sake, my religion will show me the Way.

And that is why I am a Christian.

THE MAGIC BOOK

15 May 2011

The reason the Western World has been so awed and fascinated with the Gospels is that they are not really about any thing, but rather about nothing, or no-thing. They transcend the world of objects and become carriers of ideas and a handbook for living.

The whole New Testament is another <u>kind</u> of document. It is not about how to get ahead in the world—money, power, and prestige, although there have been countless charlatans who have misused it for exactly those purposes. Some stand from a frosty distance and scoff and hurl slurs its way calling it a pack of lies.

But in the main, good folks have used it as a compass to chart their way through our confusing world. They are on the hunt for something beyond life, beyond the smugness of place and position, beyond the chains of opinion, beyond the prison of argument. This is why millions of people go to church every Sunday and will attend thousands of bible study groups around the world every week. We can't get enough of this good stuff—these mysterious concepts and ideas that we argue and mull over ad infinitum. Though the words are the same for all of us, they enter each of us differently and reflect back who we really are. That is why it is a magic book.

The Gospels especially are all about qualities, not quantities. We've always had trouble finding words from our solid world for an ethereal world, a wordless realm. To be Blessed or Forgiven is not something that can be measured. So, this is why the Gospels are bursting with metaphors, allegories, symbols, parables, and generally hard to pin down language that has no physical meaning at all. Even the word 'spirit' has an earthly root, meaning breath or air in both Latin and Greek. We have to feel our way through these concepts with borrowed linguistics. The Gospels are a breath of fresh air that brings the immaterial world to life.

That is why scholars are wasting their time studying the historical Jesus for clues to his teaching because it is timeless and placeless. 'Turn the other cheek' is not about cheeks at all but about fortitude and forgiveness. Keeping lamps lit is not about lamps at all but keeping opportunity alive. Fortitude, forgiveness, and opportunity are all emotional words, foreign to the microscope or telescope, but full of meaning to those of us who seek a deeper sense of life.

In the Gospels Christ laid out a grand puzzle for humanity to solve in order to construct a spiritual edifice that will eventually leave the body. But the pieces are hard to understand. Each piece must be contemplated and lived with internally before we can figure out how they fit together. We have five dimensions to ascertain the material world, sight, hearing, smell, touch and taste. They are data collectors only, periscopes that point outward. Unless we turn them inward and develop insight, we can understand nothing of the significant part of us, and the puzzle will remain unsolved and we will not sprout wings. These pods we are supposed to grow out of stay sealed.

The highest art is the art of self-improvement, but one must do it themselves. Even the best animal trainers can't train a man. However, the New Testament is a quiver full of arrows pointing the way to higher ground.

*

The idea of heaven has always been a difficult concept. In the regular Gospels Jesus gives parables that never relate to a place of heaven, but rather a kind of situation that creates a state or mood.

From fairly early on in my meditations of the nature of heaven I came to the conclusion that beauty and heaven merge in a lyric symmetry—the more intense the beauty, the higher the Heaven. Linguists say the original meaning of

13

heaven was 'home.' That makes sense. Christ kept inviting us home.

*

At Easter I went to the Ballet with my daughter and granddaughter to see Swan Lake. As I sat there next to those two loved ones I realized that they sprung up out of me, two saplings from my tree.

As I looked at them and then the swirling ballerina and felt the pleasant atmosphere of the auditorium, I recalled the quote in the Gospel of Thomas:

"The Kingdom of the Father
is spread out on the earth,
but people do not see it."

In those few moments I was in the Kingdom of Heaven. I could not want more. Beauty had entered me. Sitting on a cloud playing a harp as a disembodied spirit would be a poor substitute for being at the ballet that day.

Then later I was with a friend in a Mexican restaurant and had a conversation with the waiter. He told us how he got his children interested in music. He sang to them all the time. Then he bent close and sang a Mexican lullaby he had sung to them every night when they went to bed. For 3 or 4 minutes, in a clear, beautiful tenor voice he sang, just to us. All tingly, I was transported up and out of myself for that time. It couldn't have been more beautiful. It was heavenly.

*"The Kingdom of the Father
is spread out on the earth,
but people do not see it."*

*

A few weeks ago I was reading a novel and one of the characters was walking through an art museum in Amsterdam, when he passed by a self-portrait of Rembrandt at 63 years old. He commented on how ugly Rembrandt was. What made that interesting was that I own a copy of that same painting I got in 1980 on a visit to Holland and have had it in my house ever since. It has been above my bed for the last 5 years. I looked at the painting. Um…was he ugly?

I also have a picture of Abe Lincoln in my bedroom on the other wall. You should know that my walls are full of my spiritual advisors that have adopted me over the years. They are there to keep an eye on me. Anyway, Lincoln was called ugly by a variety of people. The New York Times called him a baboon, an ape, a gorilla. Um…was he ugly?

And so, ladies and gentlemen, there you have three men with deep and lasting qualities whose beauty was turned outside in. As the quantitative world wages war on our bodies, heaping us with indignities, making us sag and droop, forgetful and sluggardly, and subject to every rude wind that blows our way, let us secrete our best parts within, that trove of beauty we have accumulated, and we will live at Home—the Kingdom of the Father, forever.

THE RICH MAN IN HELL

29 September 2013

I wanted to speak for a little bit about today's gospel. The subject is hell and how no matter who tells the brother's of the rich man about its torments, they won't believe it and will keep going on their wicked way.

The story is an allegory of how humanity treats the subject of hell. Life after death <u>as</u> a function of ultimate and final justice is just not discussed among many people. They may be incapable of considering such a sorry fate. The prospect of death itself is scary enough, anything after that cannot be conceived.

Yes, hell is a hard sell because it gives us the creeps to even think about it. It is looked upon as a threat to our pleasant imaginings and hopes. It seems that our current spiritual leaders do not touch this hot topic either, even though there are many references to it in the Gospels. Even before Christ, a place of torment was an old idea. Plato introduced hell to <u>his</u> readers, and it is one of the levels in the Hindu conception of the afterlife.

But regardless what the Gospels say about hell, we use some nifty dodges to avoid facing its possibility. Liberal Christians in general hold out the idea of a free pass awarded by the Grace of a loving God. Others use the rational that Jesus died for our sins as a ransom for future bad behavior. However, the most common is the assumption that "I am a good person so I don't worry."

But in general, there seems to be few people in the whole world that take the idea of Hades seriously. There is so much crime, greed, hate, vengeance, and unceasing violence of every sort pervading the planet that the concept of eternal punishment can't be playing a very important role in how folks live their lives.

*

Well, I believe in hell. But more generally, I believe in a life after death. Now we exist in an animated suspension between the two extremes. But they are not physical.

Hell is psychological. So is heaven, by whatever name we ascribe to it. Both are spiritual states. The words Psychological and Spiritual have the exact same meaning. One has a Latin root for spirit, the other is Greek. In our culture they are used differently to try to delineate science from religion, but that is wrong. They both describe the same inner world.

In fact, if you think about it, we live as spirits right now. We are not these bodies. They are facades. We are temporary tenants nesting in these bones. How we feel and how we think is where and what we are. We are our states. Happy, sad, scared, worried, jealous, and so on, are states from which we make our lives. Our possessions and locations are almost beside the point. Life as we know it consists of a succession of such states.

Of course the states can change from moment to moment. As an example, a compliment can produce a state of elation (we are elated), but a sharp insult can generate a state of fury (we are furious). That is our temporary identity. Our states are unstable and can roil about uncontrollably from one extreme to another. Some states pass quickly through us like a stormy night, howling and booming like a cannon. Others, like apathy, lay like an old rag. During the course of our lives we do develop a pattern of states that we are known by. We carry them into the next life.

The attitudes we have produce these states. People loaded with bad attitudes fester with states like boils and blisters, creating our world of hurt.

However, with effort, we can regulate the states we live through. Self-awareness is the highest state and puts all negative states, like self-pity or envy, in neutral. We can wipe the grim off our own faces. We are capable through self-awareness of producing a high lasting spiritual state. It is difficult however. Many religions offer the tools to accomplish it, meditation, chanting, intense prayer, etc.

When we die our bodies release our Spirit. Then we wake up in one conglomerate crystallized State of our own making. This is the perpetual State that we must live with because we created it by how we dealt with our experiences and opportunities. The quality of our inner life determines our lasting circumstance. As Dante pointed out in his great allegory, there are many levels in the eternal world, a whole spectrum, from lofty to low. This mirrors the temporal world as well.

It is the ultimate justice in our unsentimental universe. By our own actions here on earth we can make the conditions for our future life. This is the meaning of Free Will.

We get incased in the States we most loved and cultivated. People who lived their lives bubbling with resentment go to the land of resentment where everyone seethes and fumes at each other. An angry man can turn a home into a hell and then have hell for a home. And also, a person who spends their time on earth in kindness and compassion lands softly among their peers. Life is not a holding pattern, but a school. We must get 'A' for effort.

Our life is presented to us as a riddle, an individual mystery to solve. The institution of religion is to help us figure out this puzzle of how to earn the highest State—Eden. Used with humility and wisdom, the New Testament is a primary ally in this effort. It is much more than just going through the motions of rituals and paying lip service to creeds. It is discovering a new road within yourself that only you can travel, away from perdition and toward the light. We are born for the heights of ourselves, not the depths.

Then, each person can hammer at his or her own private forge, shaping a radiant soul. It is a labor of Love and our primary purpose on earth—which is creating our own high destiny. Overcoming bad attitudes and negative states is our Right and our duty, but it is an uphill trudge against the grain of human nature that prefers to be in a state of denial.

*

Thus, although it is an unpopular stance in decent company, I have to agree with Abraham on this one. Even if that rich man in hell would have been allowed to warn his brothers of the misery to be found after their lives of folly, they would have shoved the advice aside for a little more of their current misbehavior. They would have preferred the wild and wide madness of wickedness of today to the uncertainty of tomorrow. Thus is the doleful human pattern.

ON NATURE
AND THE BIBLE

10 November 2013

I like to read about Nature. I read and peruse the journals, and New York Times Science section and various other sources for enlightenment on the mysteries of our Universe.

From my grandkid's 5th grade Science book I learned about bats. Up to 200,000 live here in Tucson. As summer visitors they consume over a billion insects, pollinate plant life, and then leave a big pile of guano that is the best fertilizer in Nature's cupboard.

They are little creatures that are obviously engineered to a very high level as helpmates to all those around them, especially humans. Their intricate design is something to behold. They fly by flapping their forearms and guide their movements with their long webbed fingers bending and turning in differing directions. Gargoyles in appearance, but they are angels in disguise in their benefit.

*

From the New York Times I found out that the Sahara Desert is about as big as the continental United States. It has constant windstorms that drive sand out into the Atlantic. The sand is composed of phosphorus and other vital elements that the massive kelp beds in the ocean need to grow. Tiny organisms eat the kelp and then little fish eat them, and bigger fish eat them. Eventually, that is how we come to have a tuna steak on our plates, the end of a long chain of events beginning in a pile of sand.

*

In National Geographic I discovered that we humans have countless trillions of microbes living in and on us. It is a fairly new discovery by scientists just how ubiquitous they are in our environment. We could not live without them. It is estimated that there are about 10,000 species of these microbes promoting digestion, breathing, and so on. Each species has its own job, most of which we haven't discovered yet, but if some of them go rogue or die it can be of dire consequences.

In other words, microbes are our silent, invisible partners. So are the bats our partners, and even the mighty bone dry Sahara Desert. Everything in Nature is symbiotic and intertwined in mind-bending complexity, and ultimately can be shown to service mankind in some way.

Many will say this is some incredible series of chance occurrences. I think not. The fit is too snug to be accidental. All life, from our sweet roly-poly mother earth, to the vast unbounded heavens are interlocking gears pushing faultlessly ahead. Everything has its place. Everything has its reason for being, or it wouldn't be.

*

Including the Bible. It too has its undeniable function in the life of mankind. To arrive on my table at home the Bible had to go through considerable trials during its construction over the few thousand years. There is probably not a sentence that wasn't fought over and revised many times. The Guiding Hand of Life, God, does not work with straight lines. Any Divine production confounds our elementary minds with a myriad of elaborate ruses, difficulties, and surprises. Seemingly, like a magnate at a great distance of time, it pulled itself together from many diverse places and has a life to live and give. It is a vision whose time has finally come—a bolt out of the blue that was a long time coming.

High and mighty it is, a citadel for discovery. It is the crown jewel of over two billion Christians and Jews, a literary triumph and perennial bestseller.

Yet, there are many, voices from the dungeon, who would assail its high place, chip away at its foundation, insulting its integrity, calling it a fiction foisted on a dull people, and amused at its lack of sophistication.

Well, I would like to unveil the Bible on its rightful place on that high pedestal. It is simply the greatest accumulation of wisdom and understanding ever given to Mankind. It is old Gold.

In countless locations around the country and world study groups are poring over its contents. Individuals by the millions, and places of worship by the thousands, use its words for solace and inspiration. Theologians, archeologists, linguists, and scholars of world renown discuss and fuss over its quizzical contents. Whole industries are devoted to the Bible and its dissemination. Many carry it to far lands, and under extreme rigors, translate it into obscure native tongues.

Its phrases, stories, and concepts are universally used to sooth human cares and calamities. The Bible protects and promotes pockets of sanity in our insane world, where the squabble for money and power makes us crazy.

We can live with the characters it depicts in this grand play of life. Jacob, Cain, and Eve, Paul, Mary and Judas, enchant and horrify us in turn. And of course, the heroic Jesus captivates us as he emerges from some far country out of the mist urging us to carry our own cross to that High Way. Whether we trudge up the path to Calvary with Christ or follow Moses as pioneers seeking a better land, we live the soaring life of the spirit. Jericho, Bethlehem, and Jerusalem are places in the mind, not dots on a map.

This Holy Book's impact cannot be overstated. It mysteriously binds us together whether we rail against its words, or feed on them like the Ambrosia they are. There is no getting away from the source of the Bible's power and potency. God put all the marbles in one book.

While it used to be a cottage industry to tear it from its high moorings, nowadays it has become a booming business to mock it, to parse each word for lack of logic, to discredit the stories as not being historically correct, or as the mere fairy tales of a rude ancient people. Some of its more virulent critics seem all at war with God and wave their balled fists at this solemn and sober document in open defiance. They would rip both the cornerstone and capstone of Western Civilization, and instead place a headstone, leaving us impoverished and without structure.

*

To study the physical side of the Bible and its historical context as many theologians and scientists do is to look for the trick and miss the magic. For myself, I understood this clearly when I began to think of the Bible as an idea, not an object—a capital idea that serves as a reservoir for other noble ideas.

So, this Holy Work is not a physical thing, but is a metaphysical property, a living idea, that defies the ordinary tools of measurement. The Bible is full of meaning that escapes the hard and distinctly negative appraisal. In other words, there is more here than meets the eye of the critic. The stories on the pages can lift your mind because they are aimed directly at the internal you, the eternal you. Its leaves are wings, not weights.

Think of the Bible as a huge puzzle of many seemingly disconnected pieces. If we choose pieces at random and study them we might conclude the picture itself is nonsensical. But like any puzzle, it takes patience and work to see it. It requires developing the sight of an inner eye. It will not reveal itself in a harsh light or in piecemeal.

It is for the mature and reverent mind to ferret out its covert message. Ignorance is always more full of bluster than benevolence.

*

Many of the intellectual set are hard put upon to explain the Bible's hold on so many of humanity's best minds, but its hold nonetheless is solid. This is because for those who read it and ingest its purpose they enter their own Age of Enlightenment. Those antique parables about *kings, farmers, and pearls of great price*, carry dispatches from ethereal realms in a coded language that many try to comprehend. But reason or logic is of no use here, only by contemplation and sincerity is the message received.

*

The earth is a big revolving stage, a theater in the round. It has never been a place of peace. Violence is ever with us and gives birth to our many hurts. I've heard so many people put blame on the Bible for somehow unleashing the hot passions necessary for much of the barbarous activity that is so common in our history.

But let us face it. It is <u>men</u> and their perpetual gang warfare that will use anything as pretext and excuse to destroy. For some unknown reason they are built to be the wrecking ball of life, and the Bible is handy as an alibi for masculine skullduggery, from which we are never rested.

Yes, their foul business is nature's attempt at keeping our population in check, but if the earth didn't have the Department of Men to do its dirty work, disease and natural catastrophe would have to play a larger role. Men are chemically consigned to take life and women to give birth and nurture it.

What I just said about men cannot be acknowledged officially because the façade of society would become unfixed. And nothing could be done about it anyway. We just pretend to be perplexed and surprised at each outrage.

So, it is not in the nature of our <u>Holy Book</u> to incite riot or promote torture and other assorted affronts, but some, those frosty ones, insist exactly that. They assign blame on anything convenient. Hitler or Stalin and their marching bruisers didn't consult the Bible before they roared into action.

*

Our Bible is the most interesting, the most influential tome ever written. It is the child of tranquility; a heroic poem and soothing song whose harmony of aim carries us forward and lifts us up to all the pretty prizes. Without its existence, Western Culture in any unified form could not exist. It is ballast to our ship of state.

It has garnered attention from our most educated people. They scratch their heads and give birth to one and a thousand theories as to what the Bible means, and finding little agreement no matter how hard it is studied.

However, no one can understand the Bible by going back to Galilee, or the Sinai Desert, or track back through the maze of languages, or even to unscramble the tumult over the tenets of belief among the Early Fathers. No, the Bible floats above all that. One has to reach up inside oneself to rise to its level. To ascend within is to unlock the secrets and marvels of its meaning.

*

To summarize; the natural and supernatural worlds are entwined braids. Both are required for the life we know. Nature to its tiniest quark is mechanical, obeying the laws of chemistry and physics. Super-nature is under different set laws where chemistry and physics have no sway. These are rules of thought and behavior embodied in the Bible. *Thou shalt not kill* and *love thy neighbor* are wondrous instructions for our personal and communal health.

So, we could not live without the material things of the earth like the tiny bat, the barren desert, the many hardworking microbe clans, or the swarms of creatures with a thousand shapes and sizes, without which the earth would fold in on itself. Also, to remove the non-material Biblical message would be to deprive us of warmth, vitality, and hope.

Both parts are integral to our good days. Both the physical and metaphysical are wands of magic, each with its own stage, set to confound us and delight us, and help us on our way.

And as the air and water allow for our physical lives, the Bible is the charter and chronicle to our metaphysical wellbeing. If we treat it rightly, that is, as if it was a newly discovered document, a new sunrise to our life, every reading will stir us and thrill as it brings us closer to our blest potential.

THE MAN AND THE GOD

29 November 2015

"Very truly I tell you, before Abraham was born, I am!"
-Jesus Christ, circa 30 A. D.

When I have perused the titles and content of the many books that have been written about Jesus and modern Christianity over the past 25 years or so, I have noted the push to secularize both.

In addition, no longer are certain words, like sin, hell, heaven, soul, devils and angels, in common usage among the more liberal churches, at least in this country. No such unsettling terms must penetrate sensitive ears. Word ornaments that are uplifting are much preferred. The timid idea that many leaders of Christianity are to make worship vanilla and as inoffensive as possible. They cling to the surface of life, afraid of what lies under. Spiritual practices have been turned inside out in our culture. Imposters and quacks proliferate promising <u>outward</u> vitality and vigor. Couched in terms like meditation, yoga, chanting, and mindfulness, religion has become a worship of the body and the concerns of the commerce of daily life, and in fact businesses pop up like weasels in strip malls to promote and extol the dubious virtues of mystical sounding exercise programs and life enhancing practices for success in a competitive world—a panacea for what ails you.

Jesus was none of this business. His was <u>not</u> to make us happy, or healthy, or comfortable. Indeed much of his teachings were meant to stir up our complacency and discover those things beyond the material world.

In some quarters, secular bastions, Christianity is mocked openly. The main thing is traded for the mean thing. I once read where C. S. Lewis was treated with distain and undisguised scorn by his colleagues at Oxford for his Faith. One good apple in a barrel can spoil it for all the rest.

*

I would like to traipse back to the Gospels and peer at them as if they were just now being reported by eye and ear witness accounts by people who know nothing of religion.

In this way we can see Jesus, minus the candy-sweet moralizing by clerics or the labyrinth of theological views about the historical Jesus. In other words, I want to try <u>to stay away from</u> the fictionalized and romantic version of Jesus and his aims and actions. The intellectual community that uses the logic of common sense to explain the uncommon and the unknowable has foisted them on us. Yes, Jesus had a body rooted in human nature, but also, and mostly, an authentic Divine Nature in spirit. His actual activities do not fit any conception of normal behavior. He was God, and I have that down in writing.

If we can but look upon the life of Jesus as an intentional drama, a production of highest caliber, we can enter into the spirit not of that time, but of all time. He happened to be born of a Jewish mother, but his reach was to all peoples. He was not trammeled by tradition of any sort. Christ was a peephole to things greater.

He was born in a cave, which is what the manger was in Bethlehem, out of wedlock, homeless and helpless, and was reborn in a man-made cave in Jerusalem, as the God he was. In between those two places, the womb to the tomb, the arms of his mother to the arms of a cross, barely six miles apart, came a strange and extraordinary story of a Being entering like a whirlwind in a junkshop.

*

Religion has come to depict Jesus in art, music, and words galore as meek and mild, merciful, and a humane lover and forgiver of mankind's transgressions. There are strains of that, sure, but more he showed wrath and ill temper toward the vain and pompous behavior of the so-called holy men of the day, those of the Chosen Race whose only race was for flattery and stature. Long stretches of explosive invective pepper the Gospels devoted to the vipers and hypocrites who purported to be men of the Law. He was a blast of an unwelcome trumpet. The scribes and Pharisees that challenged and tried to set snares for Jesus found to their dismay that they were tapping into a hornet's nest.

On the other hand, Jesus seemed to like the Romans. They were not his targets. He even begged God to forgive them for the crucifixion. The Centurion who asked him to heal his servant from afar received the highest praise he gave to anyone.

*

Christ was an exorcist. He believed, as I do, that there are evil spirits, demons, that take control of the body and cause the havoc world over, like the current lot of terrorists in that caldron of the Mid-East, which is a snarl of devils speared on the horns of evil. When he brought the devils out of people Jesus was all business and not nice either. *"Hold thy peace and come out of him,"* he says, while casting them into swine and sent racing into the lake.

He was also a healer of bodily ills. It is popular now for non-believers to explain away the miracles in a variety of ways. However, the people of the day, who were on the scene, including the Pharisees, seemed to be convinced.

They were right there following Jesus in large mobs beseeching his blessings and cures. There was a crescendo of mounting miracles that stunned and gladdened those he touched. There are even eye-witness accounts of the marvel of the Resurrection, which pointed to the fact that even when lying in a stone cocoon, a wing<u>ed</u> being can arise and fly.

*

Jesus brought the doctrine of immortality, which was only hinted at in older times. And with it he introduced both the torments of hell and the many mansions of his Father. He taught the <u>Divine Boomerang</u>—what you dish out, will be dished back. By our deeds do we make our selves a haven or a Hades? He said, "*and with the measure you use, it will be measured to you.*" And, '*Verily I say unto thee, Thou shalt by no means come out thence, till thou hast paid the uttermost farthing.*' I say, Ho! Christ taught righteousness, which means justice and balance, not sanctimonious proclamations. The vaunting vanity of prelates or the extreme asceticism of penitents are none of this.

He was not a politician, those great bags of wind and dust, or a quixotic social reformer. He never preached for world peace, or against war, slavery, or sex. The societal ills of Palestine were not his concern. He never advised the overthrow of any government, but instead recommended that Jews should pay their taxes. The building mood of rebellion

35

was in the air, but Jesus inhaled none of it. Also, although he advised giving to the poor, he never advocated programs to eliminate it. He said, "*The poor will always be with you.*' Neither did he esteem the filthy rich, made so by the dirty gods of silver and gold.

Jesus trumped Jewish sensibilities by telling a story about the kindness of a Samaritan, and lauding the wisdom of a woman, Mary of Bethany, over the objections of his disciples, thus stunting the war on women. He never spoke of virginity or claimed he was born of a virgin. And startlingly, he said, '*But I tell you that anyone who looks at a woman lustfully has already committed adultery with her in his heart.*' That means not only our actions, but our secret thoughts are being recorded by God. Tough stuff, this, harnessing even our mind.

Jesus was a rambling teacher, wandering from place to place without visible means of support, and as he said, with "*nowhere to lay his head.*" His charge was to spread the word from another dimension to the individual person in need of such. "*Seek ye first the Kingdom of God,*' he said. To assume Jesus had a personal life outside of his task is to assume too much.

He taught the morality of a higher world. His teachings, like '*turn the other cheek,*' and' *love your enemy*' was as curious and out of sync then as it would be in any age. He did not coddle anyone, nor did he kowtow to any earthly authority. Thorns and nails could not harness his Word. It was like trying to keep a tiger in a teacup.

I fear if Jesus reappeared in our present hardened, bickering age, his fate would be just as dire. The high priests of commerce and the lords of war would cook plots aplenty to avoid the stings of rebuke and condemnation from so high a personage.

Jesus preached that a child, out of the womb, out of the cradle, was better than an adult, and that without regaining the innocence and acceptance of our earliest youth, we are doomed. We were once sacred children, but fell into the ways of man, a besmirched chalice, by the soil of life. To do this, to become like a child again, to be *as gentle as a lamb*, is an ordinance of immense difficulty because it is a wholly internal effort and counter to the rush of ordinary life. No full baskets of hallelujahs will suffice, nor lamentations loud.

If Christ was trying to set up a popular religion, it was an almost impossible religion to live to, as hard as '*a camel going through the eye of a needle.*' '*Many are called,*' he said, '*few chosen.*' Also, '*Small is the gate and narrow the road that leads to life, and only a few find it.*' Instead, he seemed to suggest to his followers gather the sheep and sift through for the lambs that could pass through that gate—as a flock of new children.

Jesus never spoke in favor of any outward rituals, and in fact dismissed many of the common Jewish ones as impractical. Later the church that formed up in his name had to reorganize his posthumous memory into a more acceptable doctrine and adopted rites and softer teachings so the sheep would graze, and lambs might be nurtured and sent forth.

Where Jesus set the individual requirements for salvation and rebirth, Christianity was the vehicle to an international enclave of the Called, one body and one community devoted to our tender and loving natures. The Church is an asylum and preserve in the vastness of trouble, an idea of softest linen where we can rest our heads and feel safe. It is a fellowship of kindred souls providing consolation, guidance, hope, and help to the disadvantaged. From these many Called, the few shall be Chosen.

Christianity is now broken into many a franchise, and each church tends their flock in slightly different ways, but an idealistic reading of the Gospels inspires all. Jesus is a prism through which light of many colors shine. True, some are distorted, but the sparkle of God always comes through in glints and glimmers.

*

Christianity is misunderstood. It is not a thing. It is the Holy Ghost, a Spirit that holds us to a high standard in its presence. It is not the dark side of our religion that causes

38

vexation. It is the dark side of people acting out of blackest ignorance, an ink blot that stains the soul. It is man's hard-hearted nature that emerges despite the Church, and despite Jesus in the background—stubborn, sneaky and savage, coveting and conceited, easily swayed by fashion and passion. That and they are the culprits and bunglers of sweet life. People are so easily fooled and led down strange paths by outer pomp and the fiery empty words of charlatans, priests of prey and ministers of mischief, that the brand of Christianity itself is heaped with unearned scorn.

The Church is not made of hard parts, but is the nuance that nudges us tenderly and invites repose from the world of cares and strife, serenity and warmth, amidst a Godless bedlam—a footbridge across the yawning chasm of perplexity.

Christianity can help us see that all our days are laden with gifts, full with epiphanies, realizations, and insights into life's meaning and wonder.

In fine, God materialized on earth in the body of a man, Jesus, who cut a narrow path for us through the whirl and whir of lost souls. He is our personal tutor and guide through this world riddled with riddles. The harvest of all this is the Christian Church, a sturdy ethical force that keeps the Way open and serves as a refuge and sanctuary for the good and decent segment of the fold who wish to be fully realized. In this life we have Jesus <u>and</u> Christianity fused in a Holy Communion of the Blest.

So, while we as a people of Faith are increasingly timid and evasive about terms like the *immortality of the soul*, or *The Kingdom of God*, that is exactly what the God-Man, Jesus, taught in the most piercing and deep-felt terms, lending grandeur to an ever bright and living luminousness.

> *From far ago, a voice, a whisper, comes, beseeching.*
> *It is you I want little lamb.*
> *Come back, little lamb, come back.*

THE PEOPLE I LIVE WITH

26 August 2012

Whenever I go into a house I usually check out what the owners have on their walls and what books they have in their shelves. I want to know what they surround themselves with, what they put into themselves. In a way, what we put in is what we can give out.

I think that in many cases our surroundings, especially how we live, tell more about us than our words..

Some domiciles are cold and uninteresting, like a bus depot, while others emanate warmth and bespeak a vibrant history of the occupant.

*

Almost 40 years ago I started collecting paintings and pictures of my ethereal hero's. These are people who inspired me to grow in the right way, to strive for a higher life. Inspire is an interesting word. A spire is something that points upward. To expire is to die, to go to ground. To be inspired is to be pointed inward.

On my walls I have portraits of Ben Franklin, Abe Lincoln, Ralph Waldo Emerson, several of Walt Whitman, a self-portrait of Rembrandt, and Jesus on the cross. I have an etching of Sancho Panza, a fictional character I particularly admire, and many portrayals of *The Madonna and Child* because they seem to transport me to a tranquil place. Just being in the presence of people of such dignity is like having a lighthouse in the mist.

My bookshelves are of the same caliber, crammed with Shakespeare, Dickinson, Epictetus, and others of their quality. My library numbers only a few hundred volumes but there is not a humbug in the bunch. I can stand tall on any of them, and together I hope they make me a stairway to heaven.

I have two treasures I'd like to share with you. One is called 'A Treasury of Philosophy. It has short histories and longer writings from hundreds of philosophers from around the world from Abailard to Zeno, most of whom I never heard of until they shared their bounty with me. The Second is A Treasury of Traditional Wisdom. This contains thousands of quotes from hundreds of wise men and women over the centuries on every spiritual topic. This plethora of thinkers provides pithy and profound observations toward solving the mystery of life. Every sentence is a piece to the puzzle.

Now I've heard that all of these people are dead and gone, but, as it turns out, that is not true. They live still and I can prove it because they are in me. I put them there myself. Sometimes when I speak, it may sound like one voice, but that one voice is a chorus of them all harmonizing.

For me, the supernatural dimension exists. Spirits, angels, gods, and a Supreme Being are all part of my daily life. I wish to attract their attention with my good intentions. And I wish to be a product of their care and guidance. I am on a real journey, an adventure, and I am being led by the hand and heart to the destination.

Who were these people writing to? Who were they posing for, if not for me? Well, not only me. God did send all of these sainted ones and molded them for everyone's use, but few realize it. They are gifts extraordinary if we can only appreciate them for their individual contributions to humanity.

*

God has seeded this planet with people and ideas over the centuries to pull us up from our base barbarian natures. We are given these bold men and women so we could be better men and women. The Creator has endowed us with Mozart, da Vinci, Cervantes, and hundreds of others to provide relief from our brutish existence and our rude and surly world. Jesus, Shakespeare and Plato are the main pillars of civilization. They were implanted in the harsh soil of society and are still here to try to stem the tide of roiling violence that seems always to engulf us. I am proud to call them my friends.

Mankind is a species created for discord. It is a swarm of ill-will we manufacture naturally. We fight, fuss, feud and fuse together for safety. There have been a few who have risen above the din of bickering and bother. They live comfortably in my library.

*

What joy my books have brought me. They are well marked and dog-eared every one. These books built me up from nothing. I was not much till they grabbed hold of me, putty in the hands of giants. I have become a montage of their words and images.

I have every letter and poem Emily Dickinson ever wrote to me. She leads me through her garden. She explains that butterflies and buttercups, bumblebees and honeybees, blueberries and bluebirds, lighting bugs and ladybugs are God's little ministers and decorators of a grand earth. Emily and I sat on my back patio for years, minds touching, looking up, starry eyed, musing and laughing, as lovers will do.

Walt Whitman helped me be a man and pointed me to the Divine. He said to me once:

I say the whole earth and all the stars in the sky are for religion's sake.
I say no man has ever yet been half devout enough,
None has begun to think how divine he himself is, and how certain the future is.

Those were his exact words.

Ralph Waldo Emerson sat me in his wagon and hitched it to a star and reminded me '*whoso would be great must be a non-conformist.*'

And my bedtime reading for 10 years was Michel de Montaigne tutoring me in self-reflection and self-discovery.

And so on. I pay the rent for my little apartment, but I share it with a multitude.

THE GOSPEL OF LUKE

AND

OUR SECOND EDUCATION

21 July 2013

I consider the Bible the greatest book ever compiled, and the Synoptic Gospels as the very flower of that compilation. They represent the unfurling of the Teaching by which Christianity is grounded. They do not seek to establish a church with its myriad of required beliefs, but are rather the words and actions of Jesus that we all can live through to a better, more virtuous life.

Today's Gospel by Luke is a sterling example of this and I thought I'd spend some time speaking about its merits and the possibilities it holds out for us.

Luke was from Syria and a friend and physician to Paul. Paul calls him at one point his 'beloved physician.' Beloved is a good word to describe Luke as his writing, especially about Jesus, is full of love and compassion. He records Christ's last words on the cross as, *"Forgive them Father, for they know not what they do."*

He was a follower of Paul but his writings show a man who thought his own thoughts and had strong human sympathies quite different from the tough minded Paul. Luke was a man of culture and education, an historian who researched his subject and learned his facts from reliable witnesses.

He appealed to a wider more humble assemblage than did Matthew. It was Luke's allegory of the birth of Jesus that we most cherish, born in a manger and visited by common peasant sheepherders. Luke's reach is universal.

*

In our selection today, the first words are, *"Do not be afraid, little flock, for your Father has been pleased to give you the Kingdom."* Do you not feel better having heard those words? We are God's little flock of lambs. As a friend of mine pointed out recently, it is not we who seek out God, but God who seeks us out. It is the sheepherder who searches for his little lost lamb. We must make ourselves obvious in order to be found. Our lives are but a patient preparation to be recognized as worthy.

We first of all, must <u>want </u>to be discovered, and then, by a <u>special education</u>, come to understand what the Lord is looking for. The Shepherd does not want lambs that pretend to be tigers, or act like rats, or snakes in the grass, or preen like peacocks. No, He wants lambs who realize their precarious position as vulnerable and innocent, and who do not pretend otherwise by strutting and bellowing about their importance, giving grand names to their shabby deeds. Vanity has no place in God's flock.

The special education I spoke about has nothing to do with the subjects of commerce, science, or popular culture. The learning we need after we've been taught these things is to seek edification about the spiritual world—a second education for the Soul. It is the study of one's thoughts and emotions, and the contemplation over the ideas in various sacred texts we have been provided—the Bible, The Dhammapada, the Baga Vageeta, and so on. Only this kind of study will make us conspicuous to the Lord, our Shepherd. Our cries for help will be heard.

*

"Be dressed for service and have your lamps burning; be like those who are waiting for their master to return from the wedding banquet, so that they may open the door for him as soon as he comes and knocks.

Luke 12:36

This is a very powerful message and reflects other parables and teachings in other parts of the Synoptic Gospels. The idea that we must be ready and awake when our time comes is a frequent teaching in most major religious creeds and philosophies. I have here the Dhammapada, the words of the Buddha, in which the second chapter is taken up with the advice to Wake-up, Do Not Sleep.

We have been cast into a deep hypnotic sleep where we daydream our lives away, driving, walking, and a thousand other activities, all enmeshed in a fantasy of conversations and playing out fictitious scenes in our imagination. As long as we are asleep and do not maintain <u>constant internal attention</u>, we operate like machines, propelled around, not by choice, but by what happens, ever reacting to the gears of life—little boats in a big storm. To escape this truth we hibernate in the cave of our own skin, invisible beings, casting shadows on the wall, straining to believe our own show of free will.

Few there are who can grasp this. One must step out of this trance for just a few moments to see it. Then the problems of the whole world, from A to Z, can be seen as the product of this spell we've slipped under.

This is a mystery worthy of a lifetime of investigation. How a person wakes up from their stupor is, or should be, of major concern to a Christian. As Christians we are asked to give lip service to an array of curious beliefs like the Trinity or the Virgin Birth. Theologians have written many words in <u>their</u> defense, but very few have been penned about the idea of sleeping mankind. And the reason is, it is too real. It would redirect our religious odyssey in an uncomfortable direction. It is much more difficult than most will contemplate. The Way is open to all, but Jesus cautioned, *"Narrow is the gate the leads to life and few there are who find it."*

If Jesus came down to earth and specifically instructed us to wake-up from our sleep, would we do it, or attempt to do it? Well, he did exactly that and I have it in writing right here in that last line I read from Luke.

Blessed are those whom the master finds awake when he comes.

Luke 12:37

In fact, there are many luminaries who said the same thing, Plato, Shakespeare, Emerson, even Bach, a man who spent his life bringing God to our ears, wrote a song called *'Sleepers, Wake...'*

You must be ready, for the Son of Man is coming at an unexpected hour."

Luke 12:40

Who among us wishes the creature with the sickle and wearing the hoody to find us mired in hateful thoughts and petty emotions? Do we want to be caught whining and lugging all our grudges to the grave?

Of course not, our Founder envisioned a religion all about the making of mature adults, not crybabies. His last example to us should be instructive.

Jesus, perched above, with his crown of thistles and thorns, and pinned in place by spikes, died like a Man of God with charity on his lips. Can we not do the same?

A few years back I had a cousin who was retiring from the Army. He had his final physical exam and the doctors declared him a fit 45. He died of a heart attack moving into his new house a week later.

Everyone has examples of this. Truly, our next step may be our last step. To me, religion is all about getting ready for that last step. Will we waft upward or fall with a thud?

Of course there are many who don't concern themselves with such matters and may not believe in life after the death of the body. But, at the point of death, beliefs are beside the point. Dying with one's fingers crossed is a poor insurance policy.

*

I love the pomp and circumstance of our Episcopal Church, and I love our community, full of sweet people to relate to. But I don't want to confuse this with my spiritual quest for awakening. That is my internal business for which I alone am responsible.

When I take that last step, if I didn't get it right and am not awake, I will not be blessed and will have no excuses because I know what I have to do. Doing it is my own insurance policy.

That is my reading of Luke, albeit an esoteric one.

*

I just finished a book entitled A.D. 381. It is about the formation of our common beliefs. It shows that Christianity has had a rough history. It wasn't a smooth silk road to where we are today, but more like a snarl of threads that has gotten us all tangled up in resentments and self-righteousness. Blood red was the color of the fabric. The supposed saints Ambrose and Augustine were key leaders in the march to conformity. Individual initiative was squashed until Luther translated the bible 1000 years later into the vernacular and let Jesus do his own talking.

It is a puzzle how our shared religion survived at all. There was a continual carnage over beliefs and animosities between sects and churches the entirety of our one hundred generations. But then, almost the whole of humanity is still broken in shards in this tumbled down world. We have all the accoutrements of an insane asylum—anger, jealousy, hate, misunderstanding, ambition, and so on.

But none of this is Luke's fault, or some flaw in the original Teaching of Christ, which in a way has become a gargoyle of itself.

Luke's Good News to the World is a rare and exquisite work of art. By reading it we come as close to Christ and the Truth as humans can get. It is the lyrics to our longing, sweet music from on high.

THE ROOTS OF VIOLENCE

In honor of the day of infamy, 1941

7 December 2014

'It will come. Humanity must perforce prey on itself, like monsters of the deep.'

-King Lear

'A word, the lightest thing in the world, can bring the heaviest punishment from both the gods and men.

-Plato

'Blessed are the peacemakers.'

-Jesus

We seem to always be hearing the drums of war just like in 1941. The men of many nations and religions are all brawling with each other, accompanied by high-sounding slogans and oaths, and wrapped in flags and waving holy books. In some parts of the globe it seems like hordes of unnatural and deformed creatures are clawing at each other. We are living in a time of mad discord and mindless cruelty, and the trouble is we've all grown too accustomed to it. This is all we've ever known of our world.

So, as the good in us huddles together for safety, lest the wreaking ball come crashing through our own door, we wonder at the reason the world produces all this jangle of disharmony.

The culprit here is called Negative Emotions. That is a term you don't hear often, if ever, because life is so fragmented that the pieces don't come together under the proper canopy. I would like to introduce you another way of seeing these emotions; that is, by draining the dirty dishwater of our illusions.

First, I want to emphasize that I am not talking about things we might refer to as negative. That is, neutral events or situations that we may regard as negative because they don't fit into our notion of how life should be. Nor will I be speaking about people by whose nature it is to see the glass half empty. I will be talking about our reactions; our emotional reactions to life's situations. Our negative emotional reactions make a hell for everybody.

Negative emotions have many names and many levels of intensity, from griping and grumbling, envy and jealousy, to fury and hate. Each in its own way tears at the fabric of life. None contribute to its betterment. Most people are content with a life of complaining and judging, making themselves and everyone around them unsettled.

Every negative emotion is a bad guy and all carry weapons. Some, like anger, swing a mean sledgehammer, or loose a cannon ball. Others, like envy, carry little needles. Hate has a whole arsenal at its disposal, from plots to plosives. Riots and the rejection of decorum and dignity among the motley mobs are caused by these satanic emotions. Like unleashed warriors of old, frenzied degenerates hurl themselves against each other.

Now, *negativity is always about people because it is an emotion & our emotional world is exclusively about people.* Emotion connects us like gorilla-glue.

Negative emotions are not innate. We learn them from those around us. A toddler observes the actions of adults and picks up how to act and feel. Children replicate grown-ups emotional life in this way and carry on the tradition. Parents teach children by example and direct instructions how to be negative. Because they learn to be scornful and judgmental of other people children become their own worst enemy, and no friend of humanity.

Once a negative emotion takes hold of a person, imagination runs like a wild horse. It can and does often fantasize all manner of hurtful words and wiles in the comfort, confines, and safety of our head, sometimes even while in pleasant conversation with the target. So many dirty-deeds come from the cooking caldron of a demented negative imagination- -Satan's own workshop.

It may be news to most people that what makes the world go round psychologically is not love, or sex, or money. It is negativity. It is a vital, though sick part of everyday life. In almost every environment negativity thrives. We call it conflict, or competition, or politics, but, sad to say, it makes life interesting. The drama of life bristling with tension mirrors our own wish for excitement—as a springboard to hurl insults or launch missiles.

We easily recognize that the curse of destruction in the Mid-East as an outrageous assault, as negativity-gone berserk, but we are slow to acknowledge resentment, sarcasm, or bitter thoughts as <u>wee babes</u> that can grow to be giants, like falling pebbles that become an avalanche.

In our culture, we reward all kinds of negative emotions in so many subtle ways. We often praise negativity and tell stories about it in the most positive tones. Vengeance is too often held high as a righteous form of justice. It isn't, but does sate the beast in many a breast.

One thing to realize here is that violence always breeds more violence. The whole theory behind revenge is that the score will be evened out and then everybody will be happy. Not so. I know you've all heard the frequent refrain, 'I don't get mad, I get even.' This is a pendulum that swings back and forth endlessly taking all civility with it.

The media is a major culprit in teaching people the rewards of negative emotions by depicting them as things of merit, or humorous, or even noble—as a spur toward a higher goal. In TV sitcoms, sarcasm and ridicule are the main ingredients with the constant burst from a laugh track as a guide.

*

TV and movies produces most of their shows to glorify conflict. The most popular TV shows and movies are those that have violence as an important ingredient. We like it. It is entertainment. The Previews depicting people using guns guarantees a rabid and large audience. And those news stories showing Muslim brutes waving guns and cutting heads off are not news, but titillation. They warn us when scenes of carnage are coming so we will by sure to watch.

If you think about it, it is true; human life has little value. People have been slaughtering other people since the beginning without the slightest remorse.

Certainly, political leaders rarely consider the cost in human lives when assessing whether to go to war. Rather it is the object to be won or protected that looms larger. At first, war is greeted with raised fists by the warlords, the generals. Later, hand wringing and finger pointing dominate. Everyone is a Monday morning general. In this regard, it is evident to me that cosmically, the purpose of war is to bring suffering, and men's role in this is to facilitate the misery. It would be hard to prove me wrong.

*

Negative emotions are harmful drugs that are additive. They allow a person to get on their high horse and bellow against their fellow man. And nothing is sacred and no one is safe from the effects of the salvo.

*

Generally speaking, most people do not admit that they are negative without blaming someone. We will invariably point to the cause of our negativity, and it will always be another person. We will not be at fault.

The power of self-justifying is vigilant and inexhaustible. Other people are always at fault. We have been taught by society to have righteous indignation at what other people are doing and this produces the RIGHT to smolder and be tart and stinging.

Finding fault comes from pretensions that people should cleave to our standards, although we may know little of them or their situations. This is secret conceit that makes us brittle to other's foibles. If we can tap down this conceit, up will grow humility.

But, if you want to make someone suffer—insult them and you will make their day one of torment. We think we are standing on a pedestal when we criticize and embarrass, but the pedestal is upside down.

Our great negative game that we play is to hurt others by making them mad, embarrassing, or making them feel guilty. We know how to <u>injure</u> someone emotionally because we have been taught by masters. This can be especially evident in many families. Children and women are common targets by men, who can cause deep wounds. *People do know what they are doing. Everyone knows and most will pretend innocence.* We all have acts of innocence, but there is often a wolf in that soft wool.

Negative emotions of any type have only one thing in Mind—destruction. Whether it results in a nasty comment or a car bomb, its' mission is to hurt.

*

Negative feelings can spread at the speed of thought. We pass it around easily. A person could come into this room and yell something and we all could be made to be negative. On TV, we see things that can make millions of watchers negative in an instant. The Nightly News is good at this. Negativity is so powerful that someone could whisper in your ear something that could destroy your peace of mind forever.

And it might be a lie! In fact, negative emotions eat at the trough of lies and ignorance.

*

All of the world's enslavement to negativity starts on the scale of you and me. Our private gripes and judgments of others spark the fire that consumes everyone. Negative imagination, or daydreaming, is the fuel that keeps it going. We carry out imaginary arguments constantly, or replay a scene where we harangue somebody over and over like a broken record. These imaginings are practically impossible to stop and <u>eat up our lives from the inside.</u>

*

The world is awash in its own destruction, but the problem is that we cannot do anything about the worldwide conflagration. Change the world? Cure the world from beating itself to death? The world is broken and lying in tatters and strong forces prevent its reassembly. It would be like trying to make the wind go away. <u>The world will not stand for that drastic a change.</u> The Garden of Eden is gone forever. Violence in thought, word, and deed is <u>devil worship</u> and many there are who offer sacrifices at that altar.

Sometimes I wonder what god would claim us, shameless as we are.

Only individuals can put a stop to all this nonsense for themselves. Only the individual person can take the steps necessary to become truly non-violent and free from being a slave to negativity, and this means right down to our most hidden thoughts.

How can this be accomplished? The most important step is to be able to decide that we do not wish to be a normal human being—we want to be better. This is a considerable sacrifice. We will have to leave the game of life as it is now played, with its tangle of excuses for its bad behavior. More importantly, we will have to leave the game without appearing to leave the game. We must try to keep our efforts secret so we will be rewarded in secret. It is in the deep quiet of our soul where peace of mind is fostered.

After we have decided we wish to be different, we first of all need to purify ourselves of our negativity. Many religions have the wrong idea when the subject of purification comes up. They think it has something to do with fasting or rejecting sexual activity. That is high nonsense. The true meaning of purification is to rid oneself of negative emotions. Christ said it is not what goes into a person's mouth, but what comes out that defiles a person. It is a direct reflection of their inner world. To be gracious or hushed during a time of trial is to elevate oneself above the brawling, blaring masses.

What I am suggesting here is a big order. Most humans on earth cannot or will not attempt it. It is too difficult. *'Strait is the gate, and narrow is the way, which leadeth unto life, and few there be that find it.'* Any real change is difficult, but overcoming negative emotions is at the top of the list. It is a long road of many years and it starts with observing yourself as you live and think. It is like setting out to climb Mt. Everest every day. Start with forgiveness. Forgiveness is the salve in salvation. Turning the other cheek, looking the other way, is a good start.

Someone said, *'The great justice of creation is that everyone makes for themselves the conditions of their future life.'*

I would also like you all to know that we have a <u>right</u> not to be negative. That is one right we have been granted by God, but we don't know it. We got it backwards. We think that somehow we have a right <u>to be negative</u> in order to enforce our idea of justice, but that is foolish. We know nothing about justice on our level. We only know opinion.

Our life surrounds us. It follows us wherever we go. But we do not have to lug along a load of negativity in our travels. Shuck the burden and you can fly my friends. Be the feather, not the millstone. Awake to the true songs of peace within.

I hope you realize what you are hearing or reading today. It is very special and rare knowledge. And there is so much more to know.

*

If we set about working on our negative emotions, the whole web of life will respond and lend assistance. Yea!, converging angels will fly from the Divine State on festive wings to be our aids, cheering and whispering thoughts of encouragement. We will need help. We are but embryos striving for a new birth of liberty. Heaven will not allow negative emotions inside its portals. They are impure and must be purged. Otherwise they would harm the pure souls that call it home.

We were given a growl as a ball and chain from civilization. If you feel that it is time to cast off the tyranny of negative emotions; to liberate yourself from all that is bitter and harsh in-and around you, the Way is open. It is the Way of inner peace. As long as we allow ourselves to indulge in negativity, <u>we will have no peace</u>—here or hereafter.

THE TRINITY

15 June 2014

One of my favorite topics to think about is the Trinity.
The concept of the Christian Trinity started out as Father,
Mother, and Child, which was a correct construct representing
Action, Restraint and Emergence. That was from more
ancient days in various sects of Gnostics and even Cabbalists.
But as the Church became more centralized and male
dominated in the early 3rd Century the idea of the Mother was
pushed aside and it became Father, Son, & Holy Spirit.
Tertallian was the first to use the term Trinity as three persons
in one God in 210 A. D. The authority for this was from the
baptismal instructions in Matthew 28:19. However, many
scholars, including Cardinal Ratzinger and the Catholic
Encyclopedia, said it was a late revision to the text, probably
Syrian in origin.

Nevertheless, this became the norm and cast in
concrete in the first Church Councils of the 4th Century. It was
presented as a mystery and one of the core doctrines of
Christianity. The Trinity dogma became closed to our

understanding and all questioning was deemed impious. Gnostic sects (who incidentally thought of themselves as Christians) were hounded and persecuted until the sieve was cleared of heretics. Orthodoxy, that forest of petrified minds, smothered it by having the faithful repeat empty words affirming it. And so, a great curtain of ignorance closed the issue and tradition, that hard master, took its place.

*

But actually, the Trinity is a dynamic symbol and represents real processes. It is a spiritual implement God uses to create and regulate life on earth.

The knowledge of the triad is perhaps the oldest masterwork of wisdom in existence. Nearly every nation of antiquity had a Trinity doctrine. From as early as Samaria and as far away as China the idea of the Trinity was paramount in their religions. The Hindu Trinity of Brahman, Shiva, and Vishnu, created the world. With the Greeks, from Pythagoras on, this principle flourished and was called the Divine Triad, responsible for the earth's making and maintenance. The earliest theologies taught that creation was not a one-time event, but goes on eternally.

Today science is discovering that all things are atomic, that is, built on the architecture of the three headed atom; proton, the positive force; electron, the negative force; and neutron, or neutralizing force.

The triangle is the symbol of the trinity. The Star of David has two such reversed symbols, pointing up and down, meaning 'as above so below.'

*

Instead of shutting the Trinity in a box of belief, I'd like to present a more complete description of it in our everyday life.

The power of three forces combining into one pervades the Universe. The three points that flow together are called *Positive, Negative, and Neutralizing, or organizing* force. Instead of a symbol of the triangle visualize it as a three chemical compound. Because of time constraints, I want to concentrate on that third chemical of the trinity that the Church correctly labeled The Holy Spirit. It is the deciding or connecting principle. It is the catalyst that causes all change to occur and brings the other two parts of the composite into relationship. Like any compound, the whole springs to life when the last part is added. It is the most powerful force in the Universe.

I'd like you to try to set aside the notion of free will for a minute because I am going to give you another way to consider just what people can and cannot do. Along with this, try to fathom the concept that humans cannot independently go in a different direction from the path they are on. Nothing changes in our lives without the spur of the outside Divine spark of this third force. We are helpless and locked in an endless cycle of sameness until something, or some event, releases us and moves us on our way. We don't make our own decisions. We go through the motions.

To let go of our blinding illusion of control is a very great thing, but the rewards are unlimited to understanding how the world works.

Once, when I first went into the job market after college, I was stuck in a junior position that was dismaying, but because of family ties I was expected to keep it for a long time. At my lowest point I received my draft notice, and soon I was free of my burden. I began what I now think of as the start of a new life during and after the army.

Another time, I owned a business that was not only wearing me down, but putting into more debt than I ever envisioned. No way out, I thought. I could never repay what I owed. Then, one morning in January, 1994, an earthquake struck and my business was destroyed. The result of this was insurance bailed me out when things seemed darkest.

In each of these cases, an event changed everything. Accidents on our level are guiding lights on another. I was looking for a way out of my situations and opportunity unleashed the old bindings. Doors were suddenly opened, and all the equations in my life changed. We are all locked into position until we are goaded into change.

The thing about this Spiritual chemical is that it is invisible and unpredictable. It is a force, a spiritual power, that takes many disguises, but always comes from the outside. It is always a surprise when we end up where we end up. We are at the mercy of events. WE CANNOT KNOW WHAT IS GOING TO HAPPEN. And what happens determines our life. Events are not beholden to our prognostications. The First force of the Trinity is to try, to put forth an effort, but this in no way guarantees the outcome. Work toward a certain end might bias the odds of it occurring. Absent effort, we must take what is served up. Second Force is resistance, the trouble life serves up in almost everything we try. If First force is Go, the initiating force, then Second Force is Stop, or resistance. Third Force decides what happens-yes or no, and more likely a combination of the two ending in unpredictable situations and possibilities. Third Force is the engine of transformation, the spark that ignites a new fire. I can't possibly tell you what my being drafted meant to my life afterwards. Everything just fell into place. Everyone has stories like this, because life cannot run any other way.

This is a very complicated idea and requires another kind of thinking. Humdrum, everyday thinking will not do. We are not masters of our fate, but simple participants.

The message of the Trinity is that we are created from the action of three co-equal forces, mirroring the early Hindu beliefs. It has nothing to do with three persons in one God, but rather God continually spawning and nursing the world from triad building blocks.

The secret of the Trinity is tightly wound but its puzzle can be solved and understood only by watching our own life as it unfolds, not lolling about in the mirage of free choice. We can wipe the film of illusion away and replace it with illumination.

So, the Trinity is not an empty belief that church dignitaries fumble for an explanation, but a living law to be explored.

THINKING ABOUT EVIL

6 November 2011

I want to talk about the subject of evil, but do it in a variety of ways because it is not simple. We usually slap a label on a disgusting action and forget it. I would like to discuss especially the question of why there is such a thing in the first place and even why it has such a prominent and important place in human society. Like the poor, evil has always been with us. The so-called 'problem of evil' may not be that at all. Just misunderstood. It might serve an indispensible function in our world, perhaps as a balance weight that makes the good and the spectacular beauty all around us possible.

Life is a circle, not a plane. Everything comes round: day and night, winter and summer, construction and destruction, appearance and disappearance. We are not going to live or die, but live and die. It is the same with good and bad. We easily forget the good because the bad, or evil, is much more fascinating and memorable. So the problem of evil is the same as the problem of good. We have it because we must.

Mostly though today, I want to concentrate on our internal, psychological world, where evil is nestled. Evil is never out here in nature in the rumble of an earthquake or the roar of a tornado, but rather in our minds and hearts. Nature is arranged correctly. It is our inner world that is deranged.

*

God has set man down on earth full of frailties. Humans by unending example have proved less than stellar characters with their barbaric wars, petty crimes and ceaseless corruption. Indeed, life is little more than one calamity after another. We wonder why this is so, and wish it weren't so, but still go on with our merry ways that promote such behavior. Clearly, somehow we are masters of our own fate and have been <u>left alone</u> to our own devices. Still, there are those who would point an angry finger at God for allowing us to be so callous to each other when He could end all of the mischief by requiring better behavior. We want God to make everybody else behave.

Do we really wish such an existence? Do we wish that God would take a direct role in controlling us in word and deed? We would soon chafe at such supervision—and have when it has been tried by our own kind. We are not made of gentle fluff, but rough stuff. We are not sheep and we were not created to toe any line, even when God draws that line. No, we are here to make of ourselves what we will with what we are given. God throws us into the maelstrom of life and lets us stand tall or slink low.

*

Sometimes the idea of evil is very subjective. Alexander the Great conquered great swaths of land, killing perhaps millions in the process. Certainly the slaughter of so many was an evil, a high crime against humanity. However, historians agree that this conquest brought in its wake a superior, learned culture everywhere he marched. It was the catalysts for many things that can be termed good as a result of all the carnage. Flowers can grow on every grave. The term 'evil' in this case fades in a cloud of relativity. The same for any war, it seems to be nature's way of keeping the population manageable. A war is a sort of cleansing and a fresh start after the anguish and terror is gone.

*

The nature of men, their chemical makeup and rearing, guarantees that there will always be war somewhere. They are the captains of destruction. Men, away from the civilizing influence of women, must be strictly disciplined and controlled or their pugnacious natures will be unleashed. Large clusters of men, without sane leadership, are inherently unstable and easily led to howling havoc. They need the crackle of the home fires, not the campfire, to tame them.

*

Now I want to talk about evil as a living spirit. I want to define an evil spirit for you. It is not something flying around that enters our body like a ghost. <u>It is a thought or thoughts that have become deformed</u>. They take up residence in us as judgments, grow into resentments, and then morph into grotesque attitudes that can dominate our psychological and spiritual life. Thoughts are the motors that run our life, and if these evil thoughts calcify and crystallize we can become sub-human—gargoyles ready to leap.

When people talk about it in the most concrete terms they can about evil, they usually give the big, well known examples like Ide Amin or Pol Pot slaughtering thousands of innocent people. Certainly the act of callous murder is the work of evil, but what about the evildoer? Does an evil spirit just live in those people, festering like a boil, or are they one with the evil, inseparable. When we execute the evil-doer, do we kill the evil or just its carrier?

Well, certainly if we think of evil <u>as a spirit</u> then we can never kill evil, only its housing. Evil will find another host. There are many willing to carry the fiery torch.

When we put some child molester in jail, we only imprison the body. The monster lives within dormant and untouched. It can patiently wait for another chance to spring on some unsuspecting innocent. Time is of no consequence to an evil mutant who is invisible. It can fantasize ever more dastardly deeds in the interim.

73

Evil's occupation is to create havoc and suffering, not to stay out of jail. Once evil has a beachhead within a man's heart, the man is only a puppet carrying out orders from below. Evil has a job to do, a business to run, and will inhabit anybody it can if it can get in.

An evil spirit likes publicity. It makes the carrier do ever more outlandish and stupid things until he is caught by society. Then evil can preen around showing off its wicked best.

If you don't believe in devils, go to any hardcore prison and it will be full of men housing evil spirits. Listen to the noises, watch the faces contort, and feel the terror from souls congealed into dark foul masses. Maximum-security prisons are The Kingdom of Hell on earth. I taught kids from a youth prison for two years and it was frightening. I had guards in the room with me.

In his time on earth Christ threw out evil spirits from the afflicted. These were the evil spirits we are talking about. To evict them is the only way to save a person, but society has no means to do this. Harsh prisons only house and feed the evil. It is the individual in constant struggle within his inner Self that can accomplish this task. It can be the difference between the living and the lost.

*

In the American culture we bottle feed and wean these spirits on images of death and evil deeds. Our media glorifies the act of death by detailing who died and how they died. TV and movies are most popular when they depict the suffering in as graphic a devotion to wounds and blood as possible. Video games revel in various forms of butchery. And they all make money by entrancing us with visions of evil. Of course, none dare call it evil. Call it entertainment. Call it money in the bank.

There are many events we do not call evil simply because they are done to an enemy. 9/11 was certainly an evil done to America, but what about the countless bombings of civilians or mistreatment under the guise of self-defense that the U.S. has been party to? If we can give a name to an enemy, Jap, Kraut, Gook, or Terrorist, they can be regarded as less than human and deserving of our violence. America did not invent the double standard, but we have made it into a fine art.

*

It is important to understand that we humans are designed in this way. Evil has seeds planted in even the nicest gardens. Fortunately, most of it stays unnoticed under the cover and safety of our forehead. Here I'm not talking about the acts of a criminal. I'm speaking about our secret inner world, which is like the Wild West without a sheriff, our hurtful gossip, or things we imagine—the invisible arguments, scenes of subtle put-downs, or outright mayhem we practice as part of our daily inner life. The root of this is the adage, 'You can't go to jail for what you're thinking.'

Our world festers with negativity. There is something wrong with people. They, we, are attracted to bad news and disharmony. Slander and the whisper of scandal travel at the speed of sound. Newspapers would soon wilt without death and mayhem to trumpet. The business sections show we do less praying for each other and preying on each other. We live in a world of people, which is not a safe and sound place to be.

This keeps the majority in turmoil, <u>but</u> is the opportunity for a few to master themselves and rise above the din and dismay of normal human behavior. Life, in its highest and most exalted form, is about growing above the quarreling and menace that is all around us. When we go anywhere we know to be careful. In our society a graveyard is a secure place to be. It is where the living collect that villainy lurks.

Animals, and indeed all nature, are trustworthy. Every threat is upfront and gives a growl, a rattle, or bares fangs before striking. Human beings, in this regard, hide many things in the dark halls of their minds, and so often stalk and skulk around for victims before becoming bloody leapers. Evil's main prey is innocence in all its forms: children, women, the naïve, the feeble, the unsuspecting. Even Corporate America, born without a heart, can be masters of deceit in advertising and billing. They are the proud inventors of small print.

Christ asked us to judge not, but that is <u>not</u> how we were taught by society. Listen to almost any conversation and it is full of judgment of others and other's endeavors. Our complaints against each other are legion and growing. It is a gross form of recreation and the cradle of evil and leads directly to our foolish brawling.

Many a hard heart beats under a costume of respectability and merit.

Examples are many of the lamb turned wolf-man. The CEO who robs from his company, the doctor who kills his patients, the priest who abuses his altar boys, are just a few of many surprises heaped on us by our fellows. A recent study concluded that most of the false convictions that send people to prison were the result of <u>intentional</u> malfeasance on the part of the officials.

There has always been a great mistrust of our own natural sexual drives. We were given such urges to propagate our kind and provide an unmatched source of health giving pleasure. But too often sex has been used by some to produce roaring guilt, especially among many religious folk, who sometimes huddle in dark and dank cells in cloisters and austere monasteries quivering with remorse for fully natural thoughts and actions. For many men of this mind-set, the very presence of women, or a glimpse of ankle or shock of hair, is a threat to their sanctity and purity. And this is supposed to have something to do with pleasing God? It seems more like an insult to the Creator's bounty. Promoting this kind of shame under the trappings of moral authority is evil too.

*

So, evil does exist. It is in the labyrinth of everyone's life, touching us in our travels. It tempts. It beguiles. Sometimes it is thrust upon us. It is less a thing and more a continuum, from an errant thought to the actions of a tyrant. Taken only as itself, evil can seem to have no redeeming qualities. It causes unremitting sorrow.

But many times there is another side that goes unreported. In a larger sense, even good and great things flow from it as it dispenses with the old or rotten, as when wolves attack the sick and crippled of a herd and keep it robust, or one culture crushes another to make room for an enlightened way of life.

Such is the story of life on earth. And much of the bad begs understanding of its vital place on earth, not horror.

On a personal level, evil is everyone's dragon in the cave waiting to be pacified. A good deed, a kind thought, is a candle in the dark. If we surround ourselves with such lights it becomes a protective halo from the witch's brew of trouble that bubbles around our lives, and converts our mountains into molehills.

78

That is the secret of the sacred. Decency of thought and action shapes our soul, our God within, into something finally real, finely made, gentle, delicate and beautiful.

MODERN THEOLOGY

11 May 2014

Over the past 50 years or so the emphasis of Biblical scholarship seems to revolve around the historical Jesus in the era and circumstances of his life. It is an effort to make sense of the inner meaning of Jesus by searching the musty archives. That is what educational institutions and scholars are supposed to do—look at phenomena from different physical angles. There have been countless books written on the cultural reasons why Jesus said what he said.

I've studied many theories about the influences that Jesus lived under and found all of them interesting, but beside the point. None of them, whether they postulate that Jesus was enmeshed in the Roman, Greek, or the Jewish world makes a bit of difference on how to attain immortality. It seems modern Theology is lost in intellectualism. To study the historical Jesus is to discount the message, which is timeless and culture free.

Christ left a supreme legacy of teaching to follow and to live with. And there is nothing like his parables or preaching before or since. It is a deep well of Living Words that is fresh in every age, manna from another world.

I find it a bit peculiar that references to a future life is rare in our churches these days. I thought that was the whole thrust of Christianity. Without the hope of salvation from our low state I don't see a compelling reason to be a Christian. I have often wondered why someone would call themselves Christian and not believe or strive for the Celestial abode. Modern Christianity has become a marker of respectability and is listing toward secularization. Liberal Christianity is a big tent, allowing influences from many Eastern and New Age philosophies as if they bolster the pure Christian quest.

I have a large book comparing the sayings of Jesus, Buddha, Krishna, and Lao Tzu, side by side. It is an interesting effort by the author, but there really isn't any comparison between them. Christ's teachings are much more profound and specific to eternal goals than any of those others. It is a real stretch to say they are on the same level.

The thing is, Bible history is stimulating in an academic way, but never enters the sanctuary where the secrets are kept. The New Testament, especially Matthew, Mark, Luke, and Thomas, is the ultimate guidebook to Salvation. Each is a bag of treasure for the heart, not the head. The heart is the locket of the Lord.

The study of history of first century Palestine may give a certain kind of knowledge from where many conflicting theories can propagate, but like driven leavess they float further away from the tree.

*

Jesus introduced a whole new level of existence when he said we could be <u>Blessed </u>by transforming our daily lives from the barbarous to the idealist using his instructions.

He told us to be merciful, forgiving, and not to judge.

He bade us not to even think of revenge, to turn the other cheek.

And he asks us not to pray or give alms for the mere show of it.

He gave us a prayer to say that is packed with meaning.

Most of all he warned us that it is a wearisome road ahead to salvation:

Enter through the narrow gate
Wide is the gate and broad is the way
That leads to destruction
And those who enter by it are many.
For the gate is narrow and the way is hard
That leads to life
And those who find it are few.

He asked us to wake up from our dream world and through Thomas bade us to Know Ourselves above all.

Many are called, few chosen, he warned. It is far more difficult than having a little water dripped over our foreheads and think we are all set.

He told us we must have faith and we must change our thinking in order to reach the Kingdom.

These are just a few of the things to which we are advised to devote our lives. The Gospels cannot be understood in terms of this world. They greet each day with the same ancient promise of discovery and rebirth.

*

Friedrich Nietzsche famously wrote that God is dead. Often it is quoted, but always misunderstood. He had an insane person make that speech but what he meant was that it is not God that is dead, but that the people are dead to God. By our actions and attitudes we have become likened to Zombies. *"Let the dead bury the dead,"* Christ said. He is not talking about our bodies, which are molds of meat, but rather our Spirit, which can wither and die while we still move about.

*

I've had many discussions with people who believe this <u>Great Unknown</u> that we label God is an unconditional loving Deity, loving all equally, and equally headed for the Promise Land. I don't think so. I can't find that in my Bible. The parables are full of just the opposite. But what I do find is a

83

demanding God who only showers love on the ones who deserve it. '*Seek and ye shall find,*' it says. In Luke the angels sing, '*Peace on earth for those who God finds favor.*'

That is our narrow path. It is in this that our Souls, whole and hardy, speak. Our Time is now, not thousands of years ago.

ON MORTIFICATIONS OF THE BODY

27 July 2014

"I declare to you, brothers, the flesh and blood cannot inherit the kingdom of God.

–Paul, 1 Corinthians 15:5*0.*

I know someone here at church, who regularly goes on long severe fasts to bring himself closer to God. The late Pope John-Paul II was a man who engaged in self-flagellation and other mortifications of the body in imitation of the flagellation of Jesus. Starting in the 6th Century the practice among some Christians of self-scourging began. In time there were even 'lady flagellants,' and places to carry it out in semi-private called 'Flagellariums.' By the 13th Century extremists in the Church took the practice of public mortification to new lows and became a militant pilgrimage with mobs of flagellants descending on European cities. This produced a mass mania of moans across the land. A kind of hysterical dark-age of the soul descended on the land until the mid-14th Century.

Countless mystics throughout history used such practices to produce altered states they thought as holy and veritable tickets to heaven. We honor many of them with the title of Saint. For instance, one of our most revered saints, Francis of Assisi, abused his body regularly and even called it 'my donkey.' He is the patron saint of little animals, but to his sacred body he was no saint.

Since the 2nd Century men were volunteering to go live in dungeon-like monasteries. There they lived the life of a prisoner, musty dark cells, silence, unappetizing food, harsh discipline, strict rules and a regimen of work, prayers or chanting. All of this was done supposedly for the love of God. Even today, in places like Mt. Athos, the monks live spartan lives and are even forbidden to look upon the skin of a woman. They seem to think that by living sterile lives & rejecting the bounty of God's created World that it is somehow pleasing to our Maker.

What goes here? This seems like loony behavior. It is loony! It is a game of pretend, "Look at me, how I suffer and share in the rapture of Jesus." To me it is clear that self-abuse is no better than abusing someone else. In some religious circles however, it is still tolerated and even thought a virtuous calling to bash one's body in a morbid form of devotion.

Self-abuse came and was often encouraged by the powerful Catholic Church, whose bishops and abbots administered astonishing cruelty to those under them. Another Franciscan saint, Anthony of Padua, was a pioneer in the torture of his monks, using thongs, whips and rods to discipline and bestow humility for the smallest infractions. This was a time when paternalistic power ran riot. It was only natural then that people began to take it upon themselves to use the lash on their own backs in imitation of their sadistic clerics, bringing the torments of hell on earth.

*

I was doing some research into Jewish wisdom teachings for something I'm writing, and I was struck by how consistent their teaching on this was. Judaism is pointed toward optimism and a faith in a God who delights in the happiness of His creatures. To not enjoy God's gifts is the sin. Jews have suffered much in their history, but not intentionally. There is no such thing as a Jewish monastery, or much record of ritual abuse of their bodies.

There are some exceptions. The Kabala recommends fasting as a means to communion with heaven. Also there were scattered instances of disrespect for the body among the Jewish people. John the Baptist and the sect of Essenes apparently lived lives of austerity on purpose.

Jesus was said to have fasted for 40 days in preparation for his ministry. In the Bible the number 40 is used continually for a period of preparation, like the Hebrews wandering in the desert for 40 years, 40 days of Lent, and so on. There are over 140 examples of this in the Biblical Canon. The number 40 does not signify time, but rather the seriousness of the event. An actual complete fast of 40 days is possible and done many times, but not without the risk of harming ones health.

Of course, Jesus did allow his mission to be accomplished through his crucifixion, but he did try to pray his way out of it unsuccessfully. In fine, Jesus was a moderate man teaching to the inner man in all of us and not recommending unnecessary anguish.

As I have researched this phenomenon of mistreatment of the body, I have discovered that in many religions and societies, the practice of violating the sanctity of the body is commonplace. In India, especially among the Fakirs and Yogis, an odd assortment of severe self-tortures is accepted as religious practice.

*

It seems to me that to engage in such beastly behavior as self-torture is sub-human, regardless of the high-sounding motives. It is a noble thing to accept the limitations Nature has assigned one. It is ignoble to court them. Life sends plenty of suffering our way. Suffering is a universal experience. We don't have to invent our own.

Sickness, pain, and distress are no strangers in our lives. This is not a safe and sound world. We teeter on the edge of calamity regardless of our station. Endurance without complaint is angelic and our only sane remedy, but it can be long and tedious.

St. Theresa, a Carmelite nun in the 19th Century, said that the loving acceptance of life's many hardships is what is pleasing to God. She advised that instead of physical penance, a much higher calling is to foster loving relationships with others. But for some of the corporal punishment buffs, that would be much harder. It would require leaving the land of self-absorption and entering the world of kindness and care.

Our natural suffering, misfortunes, and woe of all sorts, which will come in due time, can be transformative. Taken rightly, they can actually be a boon, a lesson, and an opportunity for growth. In fact, our own troubles can make us more sensitive to others in the same situation. Our sufferings can unite us with others and soften our crust. That is why there are so many organizations that self-minister to certain kinds of troubles, like 'Twelve-Step Programs', Cancer Survivors, grieving group sessions, and so on. We can release pent-up tension and anxiety by sharing with people who understand. It is a union of comrades in need.

Of course, I realize that enduring the hardships of others is one of the easiest things to do, but once a person has suffered the same thing, a measure of compassion is possible. Then we can become more humane and caring beyond just the long faces and sorrow-filled words. I know that some religions think compassion is a high goal, and it is, but without walking in those sufferers' shoes, compassion seems hollow.

However, <u>appreciation</u>, the most heavenly of all emotions, is available to all. If we want a beautiful state of being, just listen and look through the unclouded lens of <u>appreciation</u>. There sits God. It is the real goal of our inner search. The outer, the body, is the placenta for our developing Soul, not a masochistic doll to starve, pinch, or beat and disrespect.

The world is piled high with miracles. Our job here on earth is two-fold. <u>Accept</u> our lot and <u>appreciate</u> God's lavish philanthropy all around us.

*

One thing further, I know we have been taught and simple logic tells us that we are a singularity—a single integrated person. We have been misled and it has caused all manner of difficulty. We are actually a trinity, three separate parts that make one defined Being, like a three-legged stool.

First, we have, and are, a highly sophisticated animal. When we look into the mirror or pinch ourselves, this is what we see and touch. This animal, our body, encapsulates the other two parts of us, the emotional and intellectual entities, sometimes euphemistically called the heart and head. The body is a true machine, a stimulus/response mechanism. Its only action is re-action. It is a wonder, a chemical factory of trillions of interlocking parts that breathes, digests, eliminates, and all the rest of it, all on its own.

The body is our hardware, existing in space as a carrying case for the rest of our Being. The three parts are barely aware of each other. Each thinks it is the whole. Each part has its own concerns and realms of activity remote from the others. And yet, our Being, this stool, is separate and higher than any of the parts.

Like the seat of the stool, it depends on the parts, the legs, being in balance. At the gym one can see a strutting, well-toned body, but the person may be emotionally immature and mentally undeveloped. This it like a stool with one long leg and two stubs—not a whole functioning human being. Most people are not completely balanced and tip toward the weight lifter, the poet, or the math whiz.

Our language reveals this whole unknown phenomenon that we are more than our parts. We commonly express that the body is not us, or at least not all of us. We say, "I hurt my hand," or 'I have a rash on my cheek.' The hand and cheek, we realize are not <u>us</u>, per se, but owned by us, whatever <u>us</u> is.

The same with the emotional and intellectual parts, we know we <u>have</u> emotions and thoughts, but they too are not us, but owned by us in some strange way. We say, "I am mad,' or I am thinking,' indicating we consider that we <u>are</u> those things, but it is not true. My emotional entity <u>is</u> mad, a temporary state of madness, and the intellect <u>is</u> thinking, cogitating, but neither is me, but rather a part of me.

The emotional and intellectual parts have no material substance and so cannot be detected by outside sensors like eyes or ears. They are invisible and must be experienced to know they exist. Only the individual can feel emotions, like sorrow or joy. The same with ideas, they can only be realized by the thinker. Only these two can know growth in wisdom and sanctity. The body always wilts and dies.

This Being that I spoke about that is propped up by body, head and heart, is called by various names, the Self, or the Soul, but it is not earthly in origin and one day will fly away with what it has become during its stay here on this planet. Our soul will go to its Star in glory or shame, in Divine Brilliance or with a dull thud.

*

I told you this in order to explain something about religion as it relates to self-abuse. The body cannot know religion and is oblivious to spirituality. Its concerns are about comfort and the satisfaction of its needs. No amount of discomfort, beatings, fasts, hair shirts, and so on will cause it to discover God. The body can be made to go through the motions of religion, mouth prayers, kneel, drive to church, but it means nothing. Once I saw Gene Audrey on stage make his horse Champion kneel down on his forelegs. He said Champion was being religious, but I doubt it. His heart didn't seem to be in it. It is the same with us. Our heart and mind have to be in it. There lies the gold.

Only our emotional and intellectual development can generate the vitality necessary for higher aims. So it is not our display of scars and imitation rapture, but the value and substance of our inner commitment that counts.

"In religion, the sentiment is all; the ritual and ceremony indifferent. Do not mistake the wig for the head, the clothes for the man."

-Ralph Waldo Emerson

*

THE IMORTANCE OF

STORIES

5 May 2013

This morning I celebrated Easter, which commemorates the rise of Jesus from the dead after succumbing to a most horrible death on the cross three days prior.

The act of Jesus rising from his tomb is the foundation and central tenet of all of Christianity. A man they thought they beat to death, beat death. Instead of being dead and gone, Jesus was busy building an overpass out of his tears, and across it we can scamper to a better, higher place.

Christ did the impossible. He defeated death and heralded a new era for all who came after. Because of this death defying feat the earliest followers of Jesus believed that it meant that all who profess Christianity would likewise be raised from the dead at Judgment Day. It was noted in

Ephesians that Christ said, "Awake sleepers, arise from the dead."

Also, it says in I Corinthians, *"Christ died for our sins and…on the third day he rose again according to scripture."* Now the idea that Christ died for our sins has had a long and disputed history. It was an event of substitute atonement for all humanity, regaining the grace that dis-graced Adam. Still today, to some thoughtful Christians it rings of pagan rituals where animals, and even humans, were sacrificed for a group's misconduct.

In this scenario, Jesus was replaying the Passover drama where during the Egypt captivity a lamb was sacrificed and its blood marked the doors of the Hebrews. Thus, the Angels of Death passed over them on the way to slaying the Egyptian's first born sons.

So, for Christians everywhere, Easter is the commemorative act of Christ, the Lamb of God, being sacrificed to save his people. It is the cornerstone event for our religion.

As The Acts of the Apostles tell us, after a period of 40 days of visiting and teaching his followers, Christ ascended into heaven, another signal episode for the Church

To the Jews of the day and especially the Pharisees, the act of ascension, through rare, was an accepted way for a holy person to leave the earth and go to God. Enoch, Elijah and perhaps Moses were taken up in this way. However, to rise from the dead was not accepted by any faction of the Jewish Faith, even though there is a brief mention in Daniel and again in Ezekiel 37 of God putting some dry bones back together again and bringing the bones to life, as in the words of the popular song, "*Dem Bones.*"

The Resurrection then was a uniquely Christian narrative and soon afterward became an appealing incentive for conversion. It was taught that Jesus redeemed us from our miscues with his final suffering and triumph over death. The Resurrection was the proof of his being the long awaited Messiah.

This was not the Messiah that The Jews expected, a triumphant conqueror in a flaming chariot who would free them from their oppressors. Instead, it was a Messiah who freed us from our sins, a grinding lethal tyranny. Christ was a gentle man, a hero clothed in humility. Most humans cast a shadow wherever they go. Jesus brought a flood of light to the world.

*

At the height of the early efforts to win converts to the Church, there were spawned a better educated group of men who began to think about the Resurrection and what it meant and what it left out. For the next few hundred years, these men, known as the Early Fathers, began to include non-Christian ideas to fill the gaps in the initial teaching.

The idea of immortality was at best an oblique notion before Christ. Scholars can point to references in the Old

Testament of something after death, but never as definitive as we believe today. The concept of an ever-living Soul was not in common usage.

The earliest preaching was that when the end came, which was imminent, all mankind would rise up in their bodies and be judged. The righteous would ascend in a kind of rapture at the last judgment. In 1 Thessalonians, 4:17, Paul wrote, "*The dead in Christ will be caught up in a cloud to meet the Lord in the air.*"

But the belief that the end of times was near became more untenable as it didn't seem to be in any big hurry, and more graves were turning bodies into dust.

I realize there are plenty of Christians today that still hold that position of bodies being raised up, though even there would be billions of ghoulish creatures by now. It might make the scariest movie of all time.

Luckily, more thoughtful men, Origen and others, including Augustine, were readers and students of Plato's ideas. They were better able to grasp intangibles beyond the fundamentals of the first Christians. They brought many of Platonic concepts into the Church. The most important two were the ideas of the Soul and the immortality of that Soul. In many places in the writings of Plato he refers specifically to this, as in the last book of The Republic, Socrates said, "*Haven't you realized that our Soul is immortal and never destroyed?*"

The Soul and immortality had a perfect affinity with Christ's teaching when you realize Jesus was referring to our imperishable Soul, not these mortal bodies which come to nothing in time. The destruction of the body cannot mean the destruction of the Soul anymore than the music is destroyed when the piano wears out. So, Plato, writing 400 years before the Resurrection, had a great deal to do with what is now accepted in our Christian world.

One commentator said that the idea of the Soul was the greatest revolution in human thought. It was the key to so many unsolved mysteries. We possess a singular spiritual entity that Socrates called a Soul, a Divine Presence, not a faculty or function, but a living Light—a Torch leading us to an inward life. It goes a long way explaining why we are here in the first place, and why humanity, since the dawn of time, has been lured toward spiritual quests. It is not, as some Atheists say, a great weakness in humans, but rather a crying out and yearning from a deeper treasure for recognition and reverence.

*

I do not actually know if the story that has come down to us about the death and resurrection via tongue and ink is absolutely true. What I do know is that we all live though stories. They fill our emotional world to the brim and we would be little better than sub humans without stories to hear and regale. Human life is a bustling community of storytellers and it cannot be otherwise. Monkeys do not have traditions, histories, and cultures because they do not have stories.

Ask a question of anyone and you will hear a tale. They sit at the tip of the lip ready to spill out into our lives and float among us. It is the way society functions, through story. In many ways, the quality of our lives depends on the quality of our stories. Even our Past, which is stored mostly as murky, dream-like, jumbled figments, is revived as sure-footed tales when even one image is recalled.

We remember stories because they are stored like rolls of film in our emotional mind whose only language is through pictures. If a single image is called back a whole string of pictures can follow like a moving picture show. The mental mind is not constituted like this. It only remembers symbols— numbers and words. It can recall a person's name but not their narratives of mirth or woe.

The story of Jesus is the very best picture show. A child born in a barn to poor working class parents, and then has to be secreted in a faraway land for protection, because all the king's men are after it. He matures into an extraordinary being whose exploits and words live in reverence to this day. And the end of the Jesus play is filled with a dramatic and grim demise and then the jubilation of rising from a stone grave to conquer death. In the dark hours of his vexation emerged a world of possibilities for us.

*

I mentioned I do not know how much of this story is true, but stories do not have to be true to carry a wallop if a grain of Truth is secreted inside, a seed for later harvest.

Thousands of learned people have mused and argued its many points for hundreds of decades. What is indisputable is its power to elicit good from humanity. It was something the world was hungry for, a nutrient rich doctrine, and it fed many starving souls over many lands. For every ill deed a scoffer can point to, countless good ones are done in the name of Christ.

To what extent an individual believes in the Easter story may not be important, but everyone must believe in something. Even not believing is a belief. Some people trumpet their unbelief's as if it was a badge of freedom, instead of just a dun colored lockbox.

Beliefs are the psychological framework of human life. We cannot operate a culture in any fashion without a network of beliefs, and they are grounded entirely on the stories we have ingested. Beliefs are then the father to opinions and attitudes that are the stuff of personality.

So, the whole underpinning of social intercourse is based on our beliefs. But to believe in something is to covertly realize we are not really sure, although we may bluster otherwise—that our beliefs are sure-fire knowledge. Thus, we must live to that which we only suspect and hope is true. Our beliefs and the stories they engender swirl in a shared cloud of unknowing. Sometimes I wonder how tenuous is our grip on reality, with such airy stuff as yarns and fables.

I am not talking about Faith here, which is different. Faith is a realization of an unseen intelligence that permeates and pilots all life. I have often thought that my Faith is rock solid, but my beliefs are always open to adjustment as new data comes in, or I change enough to see things differently. A passage in a book or a comment from someone may cause me to adjust my sails without altering my destination.

My Faith informs me that something ascendant and exalted happened 2000 years ago that altered the world and saved it from itself. But my beliefs may mutate on the details. If our beliefs become set in an unbreakable mold they cannot adapt to new information and we can become stilted and brittle to the verbal touch.

*

Without Easter, whether myth or miracle, no one would be here in this room. This story began a series of events not of our choosing that connected up to make our gathering possible.

In other words, our whole lives were set in motion long ago. Life is not a chaotic happenstance. We are the little puppets hoisted up by invisible strings. We bob along boasting all the while about our freedom and will, while we follow a line drawn for us long ago. We imagine we have been making our own intelligent decisions. But our choices were limited by a thousand barriers, propelled by a thousand goads, and hemmed in narrow corridors by invisible laws of Fate. Not only do people in ages past affect our lives today, the intelligence we are born with, our innate talents, and our drives, set the tone and direction of our existence now.

Izack Pearlman and Evil Kenevel had vastly different lives because their talents, circumstances and connections were different. And both were caught up in the fabric of a life not of their weaving. They could not switch roles.

Our lives are like a train ride. We sit in the Present, watching the things and events rush by without a clue as to our destination. The trip is our education if we have the eyes to see and the ears to hear. Christ kept saying, 'Watch, watch."

The Easter story, if it is true as many believe, would mean that the depot for the train is not the end of the line, but a transfer station to a better train, a first class, blue ribbon, elevated train.

CHANGE OF THINKING

10 July 2011

One word in the Gospels affected me more than any other and made my life an interesting place to be. The word was "Metanoia." It was used at least 24 times by Jesus as being necessary for redemption.

Metanoia was originally translated into the Latin and English from the Greek as 'repentance' and is usually tied to penance or atonement for sins. To a minority it is also thought to mean 'turn' or 'change you ways.' The Greek word more accurately means 'different thinking' or 'change of mind.' So, Christ was saying, 'In order to reach the Kingdom, a state of bliss, you must change your thinking.'

It must be important, I thought, a key of some sort, maybe the key to Christ's teaching. What was it? I don't think I've ever heard it preached in the pulpit.

I take the Bible very seriously and especially the Synoptic Gospels, which seems to be more about how to live a gracious and a delicate inner life than one of dogma and ritual. I treat the Bible not as a literal document, but a riddle to be solved, a tantalizing code to work out.

For instance, I noticed that each time Christ mentioned this idea of metanoia he would follow with a parable or give examples through preaching of what he was talking about. The first time he uses it in Matthew, he follows immediately with the Sermon on the Mount, which has an uncommon richness of outlook, and a method of thinking. There was nothing about guilt or accountability for past offenses.

I pondered metanoia for a long time. What was wrong with my thinking? It was everybody else's thinking that was the problem. I had everything figured out. I realized everybody thought that.

As I read and deliberated about it the more I realized that I didn't even know much about how I thought or even what it was exactly. I did have many opinions that I would trundle out in conversation, but they were all prefabs. Nothing original came out of my mouth. I seemed less thoughtful, and more thoughtless.

Is that why, I wondered, life is in such a mess, a merry-go-round of troubles? Have we all learned skewed thinking from the cradle, colored by vanity, greed, and all the rest of it. I could see that my thinking was the cause of my own torments. It was like a magnate to them. Would changing my thinking, if I could figure what it was, change my life and make me more acceptable to God?

As I went about my search I would ask others about their thinking or thoughts and I was generally met with incredulousness or some dismissive comment. It became clear to me that thinking is not thought about by anyone, much less me.

Gradually I accepted this as my mission in life, to find out what it was and then to think differently and more deeply, to celebrate metanoia. After all, one of my champions, Socrates said, "An unexamined life is not worth living." I am sure this is what he meant. Over the years, as I gently untied the bow of this idea, metanoia, a whole world popped out. It was an Open Mind and the beginning of a grand journey.

It seems to have released a great being within me, and that being's name was 'Curiosity.' What a kind but insistent voice it turned out to be, and what it can be to anyone who would venture out beyond the edge of the known mental world.

*

So, I would like to talk about this for a little while, how one goes about the project of learning to think differently and what can be seen or realized as a result. The Mind is the undiscovered country that we are tasked to explore. It is the gate to a better here and after. The Mind is the Builder.

First of all we need to grasp the magnitude of our own ignorance. We are like blind men and women moving forward using a stick. What we know is the tiniest bit of what can be known. We of course pretend otherwise, but we are mocked at every turn by our naïveté. Even the discipline of science is being swallowed-up by the Unknown. Every discovery only opens a bigger, and more complex box of mysteries.

We know little about the contents of our Mind, but by self-study, that is, subjectively, we can probe into its depths. Science can only view the brain objectively, that is, as some object or thing, and learn little of the Mind, our inmost region. Motives and character are out of the reach of objectivity. Theories of structure, function, and the whir of electronic impulses in the brain explain nothing of what we seek.

We take for granted that our thinking is correct. But many of our ideas of right and wrong produce wild judgments of others that are misplaced and hurtful. Our attitude that "I am always right," is the devil's workshop where all manner of mischief can be fabricated.

The roots and seeds of many unpleasant thoughts and emotions lie dormant in the secret kettles of our Mind. They mostly stay behind the façade of our face, but will simmer and gurgle as a strange brew that can spurt out under the flag of righteousness or just plain spite. Studying our own thoughts is the only way to ferret all of this out. Studying how we act is to observe the production we put on, not who we are. We are nestled deep in our psychological world, trying to write the hit show 'ME.'

I had a Teacher once who helped me start on this project. I was first advised to stop using clichés in writing and talking. Things like, 'bottom line,' 'going forward,' 'don't beat around the bush,' and a thousand other short-hand ways of communicating without thinking needed to come out of my conversation. The purpose was to get me to actively listen to what I was saying and what other people were saying instead of just the idea. It forced discipline to my ears and took quite a while to master.

Later, he had me take out certain words from my vocabulary for a time and work around them. Words like 'very,' 'really,' and all contractions were removed from my word list. For two years I did not say the word 'I.' That was a chore, but I learned to think everything through before I said it. It was a blessing I'm still receiving.

He also provided me with a long list of classical authors and artists who lived through the fruits of Metanoia. They make up the staff of my personal school.

The next thing I did, and to this day I try to do, is to stop the Wheel of Imagination from spinning out of control. When we awake in the morning our minds start playing scenes and having didactic conversations with all sorts of imaginary people. We walk, eat, and drive using the brain's autopilot while the Mind is on Time-out. While we are alone it is our primary source of entertainment.

I have spent a good part of my years analyzing my imaginary conversations with people. Who I talked to, what I said, and what my attitude was toward that person has gone under my personal microscope. It is the most effective tool to get to know one's thinking, but requires desire and discipline to keep it up. This exercise can provide rare peeks into the backstage area where attitudes get ready to appear in front of an audience.

Yes, imaginary talking is daydreaming, and daydreaming is not living, it is drifting through life in a daze. But by the simple exercise of knowing where we are topples those barriers and lets us live again. It just must be done over and over again. This gives space for thinking, or pondering. Then we can unveil a better selection of thoughts to think with instead of our usual one-track train. <u>Therein lies the gold</u>. Fresh thought is the engine of great change in mankind. It will scramble every complacent attitude and cocksure opinion we have. To question every belief, every reaction to life's stimuli, and to supplant old crusty mind-sets with more spiritual ones as modeled by Christ is the foundation of a new relationship with God. To seek metanoia means to live an unlikely life—to see through life's fog and walk the narrow path, one thought at a time.

<u>If</u> we can <u>set</u> our attitudes, which have become calcified by time and prejudice, beside those expressed in the Sermon on the Mount we can see to what extent our thinking must

change. But with our usual rigid, unquestioned attitudes, and the myriad of grievances we harbor, our future will not be bright with such a load to bear. If we can think differently, we can become different people inside. Many of our old problems will then vanish because they were the result by our thinking, not reality.

To be loving and meek, forgiving and merciful, and so on, is to rethink our whole lives.

We have bundles of writing by theologians and church leaders on repentance, full of strictures and repetitive behavior to atone for sin. Much of it is nonsense, passing for religious practice. The massive idea of metanoia is skimmed or skipped over. This has allowed Christianity to be misused and inner growth brought to a standstill. Foisting guilt and requiring repentance on members is much easier than encouraging Mind altering thought.

There are many other things to say about metanoia, but generally to give birth to a New Mind is to go through labor. It is the pain that leads to the Light. Enlightenment is Full Metanoia.

When we are finished with this temporary assignment here in these bodies, it is what we have become because of our thinking that counts, not how much sackcloth we have worn.

GOD'S MASTERWORK,

EARTH

4 October 2015

"The kingdom of God is in your midst."

Gospel of Luke, Chapter 17

"The kingdom of the Father is spread out on the earth, but people do not see it.

Gospel of Thomas, Saying 112.

Wouldn't it be wonderful to discover that we have been walking around in Heaven all the days of our lives, but we just didn't know it? Would it change our existence on earth if we found out that we are surrounded with the absolute best God has to offer? Would we be different, more thankful, and more joyous? Of course we would. The trouble is all of this is true, but for a reason to be discovered, earthlings have had their faculties clouded and muffled.

*

There is something in theoretical science called the Copernican Principle. In effect it says that we should assume that there is nothing special or exceptional about the time or place of Earth in the Cosmos. Or another way to say it is that humans are not here for some purpose, and there is no overriding design to the Universe. This type of thinking is the seed of the Multiverse Hypothesis, which postulates that our Universe is only one of millions or billions of Universes. This one just happens to have all of the fine-tuning necessary for life to appear. It requires extra dimensions as originally propounded by L. Ron Hubbard in his 1938 novel of fiction, 'Dangerous Dimension'.

Of course there is no evidence for any of this, or any way to test it, but it is a favored notion of the secular atheists that crowd the fields of science. However, there is much to dissuade a person of its folly if they take a look at just what we have here on earth that makes it so special.

*

Carl Sagan, the world famous astrophysics professor and a full throated fan of the Copernican Principle, had to admit in his book, Pale Blue Dot, that from two million miles out, looking back from the Voyager I Spacecraft, that, "the Earth seems to be sitting in a beam of light." Indeed, the optics were perfect for such a vision of our small planet from that far away. He thought that it just looks special, but isn't.

He further used speculative math to estimate that if there were only one planet with earth-like life per galaxy there would still be 100 billion such planets in the universe. He is oft quoted, although there is no scientific basis to it. It is airy grist for the atheist mill to prove that we are not unique.

So from Voyager our planet does appear special, but from the moon the earth is even more spectacular. It is a blue ball with swirls of white clouds circulating around it. The moon in orbit appears to be an old dry bone in comparison.

From a thousand miles up the whole panorama can be seen: blue oceans and lakes, continents in brown and green, and streams of white clouds with frequent flashes of light bursting within them. The whole globe is topped with a jaunty white cap.

From 10 miles up the colors are more vivid. Many shades of green and brown in the huge forests and high mountains cover the landscape.

At ground level a riot of colors from the whole color wheel is everywhere to be seen. Trees and plants of every description covered with flowers and fruit and in every direction are incredible vistas in shadows and light—a photographer's paradise, an artistic ecstasy.

Looking up at the one legged race of trees there are birds of a mind bending opulence of design and color.

Parrots, robins, flamingoes, cardinals, and a thousand others all have distinctive markings and tints that can boggle the eyes. They are little musicians, every one. They are light as feathers and not a feather is out of place. And when they take wing each carries a piece the blue sky on their backs, holding it aloft for all to see..

But even more stunning is just under the surface of the oceans. Bright and vibrant hues in unbelievable patterns and shapes are swimming cartoons. In warm water reefs and in fish tanks around the world can be seen Mandarin, Angel, Lion, Clown Trigger, Gold, and Koa fish, plus too many others to name. They are vision feasts.

Also in the seas of the earth are any number of head scratching oddities like the cuttlefish which can take hundreds of shapes and markings and colors, or the European eel, which is born in American salt water and swims 4,000 miles into the rivers of Europe and then swims back after ten years to mate and die, the reverse of the salmon. These are not freaks of nature, but Nature, God's finery and mystery. Every possible thing that can be imagined is present on our lands, skies, and waters. Nature is built to tight tolerances, ordered to the last detail, and organized into endless forms—and everything is connected in a rotating circle of life. Plants eat the sun and we eat them.

Even at the bottom rung of life, our population of insects is in the trillions. By last count there were over 20,000 species of ants, 54,000 spiders, and at least 400,000 different kinds of beetles. Up close they are all look like first-rate horror creatures. And every species fills a niche and any one's demise causes that part of the biosphere to collapse in on itself.

The animals that cover the earth are extraordinarily diverse, from the impossibly tall giraffe, to the very fat Hippo, to the stripped tiger and the tuxedoed penguin. The Archangel Nature is full of mirth too. Visual jokes abound. Lo, behold the platypus, the orangutan, the rhino, the kangaroo, the hyena, the raccoon, and the mighty flea. All have their place at the table, even the creatures we might not want at the party, the spider, roach, rat, crocodile, tarantula, buzzard, and so on.

In sum, the creatures of the earth, the plants and the terrain, get are dressed up and adorned to make an interesting and captivating spot in the Universe. It is all decorated and we mortals can see every bit of it, plus hear, touch, taste and smell all the other wonders of God.

*

Humans decorate <u>themselves</u>. Since the dawn of our species, we have been dressing up and embellishing ourselves for others to see. Our clothes, make-up, hairstyles and color, tattoos, jewelry and a host of other accessories, make peacocks look a little under dressed. When Adam and Eve first put on garments they discovered how nice they looked. Good for them. I can't imagine a world where everybody went around in the buff.

Nature is one gigantic fashion show, with all of the fauna and flora in on this theatrical production. Every show open with a blaze of morning light coming from East of Eden and ends on the Western horizon with the sweep of radiance slowly and spectacularly disappearing under the curtain of dark, which is then lit by a splash of star lights poking through a blackened stage.

Is this some accident or is it too obvious that it is planned out to the smallest butterfly to be for our delight? To these eyes of mine, the absolute symmetry and balance of it all bespeaks of an unknown inscrutable force that includes angelic designers, engineers, architects, decorators, artists and playwrights assembled together in <u>a</u> billions of year's experiment, pregnant from love, to birth a fat baby world, fit for both Man and the Divine.

*

I know many scientists of the Copernican persuasion that say Natural Selection, that chance based meandering process that seeks no specific outcome, is responsible. However, Nature's bounty looks too contrived to be haphazard and happenstance.

Every species of plant, insect, or animal is absolutely original, a mold apart, and each individual within that species is cast uniquely distinct (look at us!). Paleontologists say that up to 90% of species that ever moved about the earth are extinct. They didn't make the cut. Each was a tentative and temporary step to what we have now. When the Garden of Eden opened for business the globe was a veritable Jubilee of Joy.

The planet was primed. The fields were fertile, the meat was on the hoof, and the oceans and rivers were fully stocked. Only then did Man step onto the scene.

Is it too fantastic to consider that God wants a place for the brightest and best, something they built for themselves? And as supplement to all of this beauty created before we arrived, is added ornate dwellings and other plumes of show by the human minds and hands of engineers, scientists, poets, musicians, and storytellers, to put the aesthetic finishing touches on this heaven on earth, this earth in heaven. And from time to time a genius is trundled out to push the refresh button when dullness creeps in.

The diversity in humans is astounding. Our abilities and interests run the gamut from the rock climber to the brain surgeon, the warrior to the stamp collector. We are placed here on this ball of beauty for more than breeding and feeding. We are the very apex of the Divine design—to be able to use higher math to count our blessings. Indeed! We live in and on the abode of the blest.

*

But few mortals grasp this piece of Truth. This is because we were built with flaws large and coverings secure, like bandages over our eyes and muffs over our ears, so we cannot experience the entire dazzle of creation.

The birds are always singing and the sunset arrives on time every afternoon. But, we don't absorb the experiences except for brief moments, instead drift away into our heads with other concerns. We each get a taste of heaven, but it is quickly forgotten amid the bustle and rush of our lives. We are an unfinished business in a finished world.

It is not through the outer senses that heaven really comes alive. It is the inner senses, the senses of appreciation and gratitude, the fruits of wisdom, where the wide world transforms into the Kingdom of God, playground and paradise of celestial spirits. For us then, the river of enlightenment flows into us the more we realize that heaven is in our midst, not on a faraway shore. So, don't look up, look in, and then look around. We live in an answered prayer.

HOW CAN GOD BE KNOWN?

1 February 2015

"Truly I tell you, if you have faith as small as a mustard seed, you can say to this mountain, "Move from here to there," and it will move."   Jesus

"Faith is the substance of things to be hoped for, the evidence of things that appear not."   –St. Paul

I saw a poll recently that showed that our society is becoming increasingly secular with smaller numbers attending church regularly and larger numbers proclaiming to be either agnostic or atheists.

I have witnessed this trend in America and wondered on this. For the most part we are a nation who has been bred around religion and its notion of an everlasting life to come. Yet, the more prosperous we become and the longer lived, the less we seem to require moral struts and buttresses from the spiritual world. There appears to me to be three major camps concerning God, The truly spiritual on one end, the openly atheistic on the other, and in- between a sea of people who do not so much disbelieve in God and immortality as they do not care and are hostile to their discussion. Most of these are well educated but rarely reflective on their ethereal nature.

Many of this group may check off the box that says 'Religious,' but in no way live or think in that realm. The mad rush for the gods of mammon and comfort fill their minds. If there are any pronouncements on things religious it is disparaging a white bearded god and a toy heaven. Who could blame them? The primrose path of promise seems absurd, a return to the old spells of yonder days and a fairy-tale land of harps and harmony. For these folks, nothing penetrates beyond the hypnotic allure of outer life.

Before I go into my musings on this situation I'd like to explain something about two terms used in this context, belief and Faith. Belief is a broad term with many levels. A person can believe, or say they believe, many things. We cannot exist without beliefs. They are our practical guides to our behavior, our attempt to wade through ignorance. But many times, a belief can be either a bane or a boon to our wellbeing and our beliefs can be fluid and change many times. It is a human device that may have no relevance to the truth. Religious and political institutions everywhere are built on the slippery soil of belief. Beliefs of any type can make one rigid and march to strange drummers.

Faith is another thing, <u>as I shall define it</u>. It is a knowing, an understanding of an invisible world that contains beings or powers beyond our sense perceptions. Faith is not an intellectual concept, but rather an emotional one. It does not stand upon the authority of opinion, but sails above. In other words, Faith is a beautiful state of heart. It is an assumption that represents a feeling, a deep emotion that a person can live with-in. Faith is dependable and solid in times of trial, a force for the comprehension of life. Yea! Faith is a rock. Belief is sand.

In the Synoptic Gospels Faith is used often in this context, and is Christ's first requirement to life everlasting. In the Gospel of John Faith is not used at all, but the word belief is many times. John was more intent on setting up the parameters of the Church's existence and adherence to the emerging doctrine than puzzling out the actual teaching of Jesus. Faith is not Christian per se. It is the most important element in any spiritual path.

Faith is the realization that we are cradled in a vast lap of intelligence. The Celestial Mind is a mystery, piloting endless systems within systems in every direction, regulated and organized. What Beings, what laws, exist on that unseen plane is for us to discover. Faith is the vehicle of discovery.

So, how is Faith even possible amid so many temptations that keep one rooted in the temporal, and with so many scoffers that wander among us casting doubt? It is not easy. Christ said with good reason, '*Narrow is the path...*'

I think to begin to understand how one would begin to acquire Faith it is necessary to have an idea how we came about in several major stages of every increasing refinement. The first happened 14 billion years ago with the Big Bang, as it is called, an immense blast furnace that introduced the atom. The atom is the building block of all things physical, culminating at its highest point in the formation of the planet earth.

The second stage occurred several billion years ago with the emergence of the cell, a giant leap forward that allowed life, with all of its permutations, animal and vegetable, to uncoil into the most sophisticated animal of all, the human. The human, from the neck up, is a marvel of careful engineering. With finely tuned hearing, sight, smell, and taste apparatuses, coupled at its base with a marvelous voice box, it is indeed bizarrely precise and delicate. The headquarters of all this, with its incomparable armored brain, is bounded by two temples and a crown. It is as if a whole new top, with the newest revisions, was screwed onto the trunk of a lower animal. The Sphinx—body of an animal, head of a god, represented us in olden times.

So, from the ground-worm up, we emerged with our five senses, each showing a different dimension of a sensational planet. The purpose of all of this is to give us the equipment to experience our paradise, where the seemingly common gives way on close inspection to the most delicate and inscrutable. Taken from Adam, it is ours to regain. Beauty swirls all around us. God is calling, saying *"PLEASE NOTICE."* The wordless state of Awe is the first step to Faith. The second is not to forget it.

The final stage and pinnacle of the creation cycle is that we are imbued with a spiritual component we call by various names: the soul, the self, the mind, or spirit. This is our Being. We are Human Beings, or Man in its fullest sense. Being is not only a title, but also the princely process of rising above our animal natures. The life we are given as Beings serves as a sifter in reverse. The coarse fall to the lower regions with a clunk. The finer floats up to the light.

Each preceding level can explain none of these great revolutions, from nothing to material, from inert material to the living, from life to the human, and the human to a Being of extraordinary possibilities. They came about we know not how. Words and phrases used by unbelievers like evolution, random forces, or the fantastical 'multiverse' theory, are clever inventions designed as hidey-holes from the uncomfortable truth. But to one who suspects these easy answers are only patches over a chasm of emptiness, it causes profound befuddlement.

*

The greatest leap forward is from animals to human. How can we be sure our Being is more than our animal cousins, but is indeed boundless in potential? Well, animals are predictable machines. They do their job and no other. They live in the jungle or the plain in relative peace and harmony.

Each person, on the other hand, is a unique individual and very unpredictable. Our achievements and misadventures are legion. From the high intentioned Handel's Messiah to Hitler's death camps or other great sinkholes of humanity, we belie our lower animal nature. An animal's simple innocence is not ours to share. They always mind their own business. Not so us. We are always up in everybody else's business. God made a nosey crowd when we were made. Also, we have a multitude of superlative, intangible features, compassion, altruism, generosity, empathy, and so on, that are foreign to any other creature.

There are many levels to a human's <u>Being</u>, from the vicious to the virtuous. Acts of kindness, contemplation, and all forms of art can awaken a higher level of Being in us. A person can have great knowledge, be able to cite large tracts of literature or do complex math problems, but still be a liar, a cheat, be mean and envious. They have a lower level of Being than a simple honest tradesman or a gentle bridesmaid. Heaven does notice such things.

A person's Being matters. We gather around those of similar level of Being—gangsters with gangsters, the good with the good. In society generally, there is a mix of many levels of Being, creating a need for cops and courts. The world has always suffered from too many smart men with low levels of Being leading us to ruin. Suits and holy robes do not guarantee a high level of Being.

*

We all have a spiritual nature that comes courtesy of our exclusive equipment that is connected to another dimension. Profound thoughts and emotions stir us to our nucleus. We each manifest our high nature in a variety of ways, none of which a plant or animal would do. A dog can be taught to sit, but it will never sit and wonder why.

Is this not curious? Do you not ever wonder about how we became so unique? Was it some accident, or a plan beyond our range?

*

My thesis is that man is created from the dust of the earth to be a link and bridge to a Divine existence. This is the meaning and purpose of life on earth. Understand your meaning and there will be your Faith.

There are those who say humans have no meaning, that life has no purpose. They are called 'materialists,' or 'naturalists' and say we are here because of coincidences piled to the sky. They insist that there is no reason beyond serendipity that we exist at all., that we are <u>too minute</u> in a gigantic universe to count for much.

They are funny ones. To them everything is for naught. Everything is hollow. Those ones say when we die everything we stood for, lived for, evaporates into the ether unheralded and unnoted. They stake their lives on a mistake.

It is easy to see why this is. To such as they, scientific enquiry cannot extend beyond death, and so a life after the physical part succumbs cannot be imagined. But Faith can go where no science dare poke. Faith is made of the stuff of understanding, which is beyond the reach of the unfaithful.

The great atheists of the 20th Century, Stalin, Hitler, Mao, and Pol Pot, showed us to what lengths some people without Faith can go <u>if</u> given the right circumstances to carry out their wishes without restraint. In Plato's 'Republic' there is a story called the '*Ring of Gyges,* about a boy who found a magic ring that could make a person invisible. He used its power to commit a series of crimes. A preacher once told me that the difference between the oppressed and the oppressor is opportunity.

I believe that. <u>Too little</u> Faith can be a dangerous thing in the wrong hands. Faith is the perfect antidote to a world gone mad. It alone <u>cannot</u> be swayed or corrupted by unsavory forces. Beliefs, on the other hand, can be as unstable as a lone leaf in a windstorm.

*

Please consider that the Gods use us as channels for a host of blessings. The clearest example of this is in the sprinkling of geniuses' born to humanity. I am quite familiar with the biographies of a number of them, Bach, Beethoven, Mozart, Michelangelo, and so on. Their job was to bring forth out of themselves incomparable beauty to help becalm the rough sea of our souls. Of course these giants <u>had no choice</u> in the matter. They were bursting to produce their assigned lot before they died, thus adding to the store of humanity.

So it is with all of us. Each of us has some degree of talent, a service to render, or even a small bit of genius for the pot. Even a drop of genius can make a big splash on earth that is so parched for enrichment. But people can be so smug about their positions and accomplishments. From a high source they are given their intelligence, talent, drive, and opportunities. The only thing they can really claim is the credit.

To begin to grasp that there is a God that Faith does herald, begin by looking around and seeing that we are all molded from conception to fit into a dazzling ornate pattern. The smallest insect or berry has a reason, a right, and a responsibility to be here, just like we do.

Faith is that mustard seed. If we make ourselves fertile ground it will sprout and expand in us. And then when these earthly vessels release us finally we can slip away into the Mind of God for a new adventure that our Faith has bought us.

ON IMAGINATION

6 September 2015

Pindar, the ancient lyric poet from Thebes, Greece, told a story about the beginning of the world. Zeus was holding a celebration for his gods who had created the earth. He asked them what gift he could give them to beautify their lives. They asked him for beings that could record all the great things of existence.

Zeus gave them poets, storytellers, musicians, and artists.

As a storyteller I have perhaps 200 tales to tell. A few are absolutely true. Most are partially true, and some are pure fancy. All of them required my imagination to put together. And that is a proper use of imagination. Imagination is a subject that comes up periodically, but there is much confusion about the concept, so I thought I'd try to clarify it and its many sides.

The First Lord of Thought, Socrates, always began his dialogues by insisting that the words and terms be defined or else everybody would be flaying past each other in the dark with different definitions. So, I will define imagination as '*mind activity using conjured up images.*' We also call this a type of 'thinking.'

*

First of all know that the body is a marvel of ingenuity and engineering made from the raw materials of earth. It operates completely automatically from the time we are born till we pass on. The brain, a mound of high-grade meat, is the master organ, must be on duty the whole time, regulating every function and every cell in the body. With approximately 100 billion neurons, it is a physical wonder in all its particulars, but paltry compared to the richness of the Mind.

Astride this marvelous brain is attached an invisible Mind, a Celestial Plant and part of a great Being released into the body. It can grow or wither depending on how and if it is used. A Mind needs the brain and the rest of the body in order to operate. It is like a light bulb needs the electronic apparatus in order to shine. The Mind cannot operate without the brain. They are a matched set, like the bulb and the socket. Combined with the brain the Mind can manifest consciousness or intelligence. So, inside each of our heads are two worlds—finite and infinity.

Man, then, is a supernatural being, a creative creature par excellence because it has a Mind. Through good use of the Mind we can become a better person in the same body. So, in a way, the Mind is our spiritual child to mature or keep as a runt. Life can be a symphony or a cacophony, depending on how we use it. But, the Mind does not occupy space and only the owner can know his own Mind and take the blame or credit for its utilization.

The Mind bests the brain in complexity by an infinite factor because it carries with it the purposes and capacity of the Eternal Mind. It is but a spiritual force that seeks embodiment, filling the recipient with a host of qualities not present in the brain. A brain can store sensations by the billions, but only the Mind can organize these sensations into memories and all their ramifications, like mystical associations and complex emotions. A Mind can appreciate great works of art, give us reason to cry, laugh or even make mischief.

The brain can store the capacity to do math, spell, type, or win at Jeopardy, but the Mind gives us the reason to do those things. Coming from the land of the unborn we are little animals until the Mind begins to emerge. We then begin to comprehend the intangible: sympathy, sarcasm, humor, and so on.

The Mind also has something like a dimmer switch that regulates how much light, or awareness, it manifests. In bed at night the dimmer is way down and produces only a discordance of odd dreams and associations. When we awake from this sleep the Mind turns up a bit, but we still are in dreams, but of a different sort because we have to respond to all manner of stimuli.

Most of Man's psychic life is taken up with inner talking to imaginary people, living or fictitious. If you watch your thoughts for a while you will notice how much we lecture, explain, and entertain our fellow man in our heads. And if we are angry with someone, their picture will keep reappearing as we berate them behind the shroud of our eyes. It is almost impossible to stop this type of Mind activity and most of it is like being in idle gear. It rolls on automatically and will jump from subject to subject like a grasshopper. We can never truly be alone with this selection of people quietly listening to our opinions and rants.

Most imagination is basically useless because without great discipline we have no control over this soundless monologue. We don't even know it is happening. It is a big secret, even from our selves. We are oblivious to it until we are told and then observe it ourselves. We may call it thinking but is more like drifting in fantasia, a hypnotic trance. This is the esoteric meaning of Christ's admonishment that we are asleep and need to wake-up. Our opinions are only imagination with the pretense of truth.

It is called imagination because we see an image in our heads and talk to it as if it is there. Everyone knows there is something wrong with mankind. We seem to be tales told by madmen and ogres. If our history of crime and violence is not evidence enough, then look to modern daily life with its endless puffery, whining, and general idiocy—a rolling calamity. The main reason for this is that most of our time is caught up in a dark forest of images that we take for real. Living in imagination is like going through the world with a blind man's stick. The future is the land of the forever mirage—we can only imagine it.

But there are other kinds of imagination that are of more use and, in fact, essential to the growth of the individual and civilization.

One is called, Directed or Creative Imagination. This is when we are actually thinking along certain focused lines to come up with a story, experiment, writing a poem, or solving some problem. We need those images to help form concepts, or in my case, to see characters or imaginary situations. No artistic project or scientific experiment or philosophical musing can come about in any other way. This is a rare use of the Mind, but powerful if it does get used. We join with God as co-creators, but only if we can focus our imagination in this way. This is what most people consider as imagination. It is the kind of imagination where our attention is less prone to wander away with every passing stimulus and requires concentration, something daydreaming can never accomplish. We can only control the Mind with interest and curiosity. They are the focusing agents.

Another kind of imagination that is appropriate for anyone, especially children, is imagining along with a told or read story. It is a prime educator of people. Just like you might imagine along with my story; thus every story should elicit the same kind of mental response. If I am reading a book and it doesn't let me do that because it is poorly written, or the images it creates in my head are unpleasant I put the book down. I don't want to see those things. If I were to start to describe a grisly murder, you might stop me and say, 'I don't want to hear that.' What is really meant is you don't want to see that in your head. It might sear itself into you and leave an indelible mark.

Also, introspection, that deep absorption and musing on images is a rare and important mind activity that can produce a thoughtful life.

*

Perhaps it was the Indians who first talked about everyone living in a world of imagination or illusion, calling it 'Maya.' However it was Plato who described it best in his Allegory of the Cave. We are people staring at shadows taking them for reality and living our lives in and from the shadows, figments of our imagination.

*

This is not to say that illusions are not <u>in a sense</u> real. Those shadows on the wall and in our heads make us do all sorts of things: start wars, get divorces, commit suicide, and so on. This is because above all, we believe our illusions; that attacking Iraq is a good thing, that the pain in my stomach means I have some dread disease, or nobody likes me. So, in most cases the world of phantoms is the world that motivates us. Without knowing their source we spin and bob in a sea of imagination, talking to invisible people, or playing out scenarios of every type, and all this while driving a car or just sitting quietly in a lounge chair, or listening to a boring lecture. The silhouettes seem so real. The dominant illusion of course is that we have no illusions.

That is why everything in the world is a hopeless tangle, a labyrinth of no end. Problems are never solved. A shadow of trouble seems to fade only to reemerge in another shape and shade. We live amid hallucinations. Despite our outward countenance of calm and confidence, confusion reigns because everyone has their own private images, or shadows, to content with internally.

*

But this is one of those proverbial double-edged swords. Illusions protect us too. Would you want to suddenly be thrown into rude Reality without the benefit of the filters and buffers of imagination? We should go mad. We need many things to be hidden for our own sake. So, much of the time we misconstrue reality for own benefit and safety. Society would quickly fall apart if Truth was unfurled for us and we could see what everyone thinks, and even spy into the future. Our lives would be pretty unsettling. They might sputter to a halt from too much candied sincerity.

But in another way, if we can ever so slowly uncover the false, the imaginary, we could have a real life. The visions in our head would be crystal clear and true. We would awaken and become a prophet, seeing into the deep Present.

This is a very complicated subject and hard to explain in a few minutes. There is much more to thinking, or mind activity, than what I described. I have spent the better part of my life uncovering its secrets.

Just know that we are not at all what we suppose or pretend. Our faces and words hide the best and worst of us. Our imagination is both help and hindrance, depending on whether we use it, or it uses us. Our very life is on the line here. The Mind can be a magic carpet to waft us to a high plateau of ourselves, or a trap door dropping us to the basement of our potential.

GOD'S GRAND EXPERIMENT!

14 September 2014

"Everyone of us is like a man who sees things in a dream and thinks that he knows them perfectly and then wakes up to find that he knows nothing."

–Plato

"The Almighty has His own purposes." A. Lincoln

"The earth is a laboratory and we are the experiments." – George Gurdjieff

Last month I met four individuals who were committed to learning and teaching languages. Between them they knew 16 different tongues, ancient and modern. Each told me that they were drawn to language by some unexplainable interior force.

Also, I read recently about two math geniuses that could do equations before they were five..

In history we have had great composers like Bach, Beethoven and Mozart who were born to create stupendous music. Like so many others in their field, and the math whizzes, the linguists, engineers, scientists, explorers and artists of every sort, appear as if implanted here on earth. All told, they make our living globe an interesting place to ride around on. But then, each person alive is unique and the aggregate of all our talents fits a jumbo jigsaw puzzle, a dazzling orchestra when everyone is in tune, and not just tooting their own horn.

None of us chose our abilities. They were just there and impossible to ignore. Like multi-colored light bulbs, we were plugged in so as to bring light to the world. To me, this points to one universal truth--we are here for a reason, not just one reason, but many, many reasons. We are not here to just mill around until we die.

*

Many of us have suspected that we have a reason for being, a task to perform, and are not just dumped out of some mindless evolutionary maw to no purpose. It all has been carefully planned in advance. But we are kept ignorant of the Divine blueprint because the mill of life churns on and we get caught up in the personal storms and cares of our lives. It is hard to stop and consider such things because the racket of events pours through the Present like a bursting water main. That too is in the scheme.

It is true that we seem to live in a faltering civilization that lurches from one tragedy to the next until they stack up beyond our comprehension. It feels as if we are tethered to a sinking boat. Or it is like the whole world is wandering in the dark forest of a fairy tale full of terrors, diseases, and fiery fiends leaping out at us.

But at the same time there is an undeniable arrow of progress in our mastery of the external world. Despite forever slogging through a quicksand of troubles, humanity is inching ever forward in physical convenience and discovery. So, with one foot people are sinking into the abyss and with the other scaling Mt. Olympus. Surely, one of God's experiments is how to build a viable and vibrant civilization from scratch with a people with such ill-tempered and stubborn dispositions. That is the story of the Old Testament. Every era we are provided a fresh crop of geniuses to further lift us up to match the downward jerk of the vermin in human suits. All fit in their places, some works of art in progress, some flailing and tearing at the brightest and the best.

*

Setting that aside for a moment, it is our individual gifts, our talents, which lead us into the world. Discovering and nurturing our endowments is how we find our true place and mission in life. Also, it is all there in the syllabus of life prepared by Jesus, Buddha, Plato, Shakespeare, and others.

Each of us is born with a light, a searchlight that can guide us through the dark places of life, this is our special gift sent from our great and grand ancestor God. Some lights prove to have more wattage than others, but none are insignificant, and all important to a fully enlightened world.

*

Humans are herd animals and more comfortable in clusters. We are corralled by beliefs that fence us in by incessant indoctrination by the big bad wolfs with glib, wily tongues. Like sheep, most people wish the safety of organizations with their strict dogmas that provide pre-formed attitudes. This leads to a mass docile mental existence, not a living individual one. Rigor mortis sets in and humanity becomes like walking, talking zombies.

To live deliberately as individuals and break from the mob means to think for ourselves. It is an art, but not a painless art learning to think for ourselves and above the madding crowd. Our normal rigid mental patterns do not submit freely to flexibility and freedom of flight. Christ asked us to develop metanoia, meaning new thinking, as the way to stem the tide of ignorance that so pervades our mindless actions. I know that is hard to imagine that our thinking might

140

be suspect in any way. It is always all the other people who have gone awry.

Actual thinking, contemplating, pondering, or reflecting is all calling upon the invisible universe of Mind. This is the incomprehensible Mind of our Founder. From this immense reservoir immortal ideas can be thought up. This is the same invisible source that our greatest thinkers drew from. This invisible pool is the strut that holds up the visible. Everything done or said requires unseen mental activity.

*

I want to shift gears for a moment. The material world we experience is indeed a wonder, full of baroque forces and a swarm, a flourish, of creatures of every size, shape, and color, and all symmetrical and symbiotic. It is a world nobly furnished, fit for kings—and queens, and all courtesy of our five senses, each of which was given gratis.

However, that is only the surface. Roiling just under the sparkle and spangle of the material world is an ethereal place beyond the reach of the five senses—the spiritual world. We recognize ourselves by our externals, our skin shell with tufts of hair, but we <u>are</u> our internals, our emotions and thoughts, like the air that fills the balloon.

We are spiritual beings and our thoughts and emotions are the entirety of our spiritual world. I think of each thought and each emotion is a separate spirit. They certainly seem to fit the description of spirits. Every one of them is invisible but has a distinct and clear voice heard only by the person experiencing them. We are kept from realizing this because each spirit engulfs us in turn. We become one with the thought or emotion and are in it, swallowed, for its duration. They also provide an unending variety of visions—daydreams and night dreams.

We usually think of visions as holy apparitions, but they are everyday occurrences. Visions are vivid projections of images that thrust themselves in front of our Mind's eye in a constant loop. We don't realize their power to guide or misguide our lives in a myriad of ways. In Plato's Republic, his cave was filled with shadows, visions that the people took as realities.

They are part of our imagination and imagination has no limits. We can be or do anything we want in our imaginations, advise politicians, silently pummel anyone we don't agree with, or concoct wild schemes and tramp around and roar like mighty paper tigers, and all in the safety of our heads while staring off into space.

We have many emotions. They permeate almost everything we do or say. People who appear not to be emotional, especially men, are just insensitive and perhaps afraid. But they have plenty of emotion percolating under their apparent coolness. <u>Emotion is civilization's main propellant</u>.

Of course most emotions are like whiffs of air passing through us without laying a claim to our lives. But when we allow one of them tenancy we cannot escape its grasp. We are slaves to its demands, whether for good or ill. If they last, they become emotional <u>states</u> from where we see the world. Bright or brooding moods are states of emotion. The visions they stir up are quite different, but always usher us into the shadows.

Thoughts and emotions are quite separate and not often friends, but very often work in tandem, supporting each other. For instance, an ornery thought will produce an ornery emotion, or an irrational emotion will often will be bolstered by a logical reason for it. However in many cases they will be at odds. The intellect may realize that it is ill advised to do something, like buying an expensive item on credit, or pursuing an unavailable man or women, but the heart, the emotions, will overrule its compatriot. It is like the emotional sack springs a leak and a flood of emotion drowns out reason. Who can think straight when overwhelmed with ecstasy or hate?

Much of what we label thinking is only inner talking to an invisible audience. We are kind of a secret automatic blabber machine spitting out a jumble of thoughts and emotions. The Mind, as separate from the brain, is the source of both thoughts and emotions, only having different architectures with different functions, much like vision and hearing are different, but in the same head.

If you watch your mind work for even a few minutes you will see these spirits operating and you can't stop them for more than a few seconds. No doubt you will notice that the mind continually jumps around and rarely lights on a subject for long before another thought or emotion yanks you away to another imaginary scene or conversation, all of them figments of reality—illusions.

Our internal chatter is deafening. Because of it, we lack the ears to hear the Truth, as Christ said. In the Bible Jesus healed this deafness and the dumbness that always comes with it.

Within our psychology are many levels, from the chaotic basement of greed, and malice to the high places of kindness and patience. Which ever of these most dominate our life is what we are, regardless of our outer demeanor.

*

The Celestial world has gone to a great deal of trouble to design and build this complex world for reasons we cannot comprehend. Plato was right. We know nothing. Maybe we can know a little. We have hints that are spread around in plain sight, but we have little regard for them. In the Gospels, Jesus says over and over again, that the goal is the Kingdom of God, however it is not only extremely difficult but few are chosen for arrival at that high port. The payment is too steep for most. It includes escaping our imaginary world of shadows.

The earth is a boot camp for sleepers mired in daydreams. The trumpets are sounding. *'Be Alive!"* is the call. *"Go on a secret mission." "Discover a Kingdom."* It is not far. It is within reach. Just lift your Mind <u>up</u>. The Kingdom does not live in some far off region, but in Faith, that most hidden of all spirits deep within those of us that can find it. *'Seek and you will find,'* Christ said. This is the Holy Spirit of Faith that leads to the Celestial State of our secret yearning. This is at the doorstep of the many mansions of the Lord.

Our mission, should we accept it, is to develop enough Faith that when we pass on we will be enfolded with the rest of the Faithfull. This is the purpose of <u>God's Grand Experiment</u>, converting lead into gold, humans into angels.

A MOST UNCOMFORTABLE
GOSPEL

April 26, 2015

*O imagination, go away. In God's name thou camest,
but I desire thee not! But thou art come according to thine
ancient wont. I bear thee no malice; only depart from me.*

-Marcus Aurelius, circa 160 A. D.

"Let me know myself, Lord, and I shall know Thee."

-St. Augustine, circa 400
A. D.

In the middle part of last century two peasants in Egypt
dug up several earthen jars that they hoped contained gold.
But instead they contained a treasure that a hundred such
weights in gold could not have bought. The find contained 52
early Christian and religious texts, most of which were not
known. Among them were the incomparable Gospel of

Thomas and a few associated manuscripts of intense interest to those of us who relish the life and words of Jesus.

All of these must have been buried long ago to escape the official Catholic Church's destruction, since they had been sanctioned and condemned for various reasons, mostly because they ran aground of accepted beliefs established in several important Church Councils.

I've been reading these materials off and on, especially the Gospel of Thomas, for a long time. Many theologians have come up with logical sounding time-frames and circumstances surrounding them. I am familiar with some of this literature. Recently, a friend sent me a chapter on this Gospel by Elaine Pagels. I was overwhelmed by the detail and thought that went into her analysis and the undertone of deep faith. But I am still more moved by my own reactions to the words and ideas in Thomas as I read them for myself than other's commentaries.

What I do feel is that the Gospel of Thomas, The Book of Thomas, and to a lesser extent, The Secret Book of James, contains the most unvarnished teachings of our Jesus in cryptic form. Unlike the Synoptic Gospels, these are unencumbered by stories that carry us along through various situations, from birth to death. They are linked by nothing except the flow of wisdom of our Lord.

These writings are the Rules of God's Realm, no matter who wrote them down or when. The sayings mirror to a great extent the Canon Gospels, and in fact, may have been a source of them, but for me at least, is more compact and hard hitting than the Christian softened ones.

I thought I would read some of them from "The Secret Teachings of Jesus,' translated by Marvin W. Meyer, and make brief commentary and then we can talk about each one as we see fit.

Page 3. James writes about the construction of the proto-gospels, starting as recollections of the Apostles. I have never read anything like this before. This may explain why the Synoptic Gospels are so alike. It was not a separate "Q" document, but an actual sharing of memories among the disciples right after the death of Jesus while they were fresh, and they reached their final form decades later under the names of the men who began them. John's Gospel, which we know came long after the others, did not have a participant in this forum, and was quite different.

Chapter 1: 7-'*The twelve disciples were all sitting together, recollecting what the Savior had said to each of us, secretly or openly, and organizing our recollections into books. I, for my part, was also writing my book.*'

Pages, 4, 8, 9, 38, 48. The idea that man has been cast into a deep sleep of illusion and imagination is almost never emphasized from the pulpit or any bible study. And yet, Christ speaks of it often in the direst terms in the Gospels on how we must come out of this fairyland state, carrying on imaginary conversations and endless fictitious and whimsical scenes in our heads.

In addition, this idea of man's hypnotic sleep is part of most major religious and philosophical systems before and after Christ's time here. It was a fact of life for anyone wishing to understand humanity and its Maker.

I am not talking about deep thought on one subject or creative imagination. I'm speaking about the make-believe world, the play-acting pretend existence, we live in our heads where we are the main characters, always in the right or always misunderstood.

To wake up from this state is designed to be difficult, maybe the most difficult task in the world. We are ensnared in this cycle of daydreaming. Just emerging out into the world of the Present for a few moments can be a revelation, like pulling your head out of a bucket of water, but then we are sucked right back into the swirl of our private little worlds. Imagination is an escape hatch from the reality of our daily lives. It affects everyone equally.

Over the centuries, many monks, nuns, and other deeply spiritual individuals, practiced various methods of awakening of the Self, called watchfulness, mindfulness, meditation, deep attention, Remembrance of God, the Jesus Prayer, and of late, Centering Prayer. My own personal practice is called 'Self-Remembering,' a method of dividing attention between my inner and outer world. I have been at this for over 40 years.

In the five volume Philokalia, which is a record of monastic personal reflections on the contemplative life over a span of 1500 years in the Greek and Russian speaking world, is a chronicle of individual struggles to bring God into one's Presence, that is to wake-up. This is some of the purest and most practical spiritual writing I've ever encountered. Its thrust is the pursuit of self-consciousness and humility.

Chapter 2: 3-'*Your hearts are drunk. Do you not want to be sober?*'

(Drunk and sober are metaphors for sleeping and awake.)

Chapter 5:1-'*For this reason I tell you: live soberly.*'

Chapter 6:3; '*Why do you sleep when from the beginning you should have been awake that the Kingdom of Heaven might receive you?*'

Saying 112- *'The Kingdom of the Father is spread out on the earth, but people do not see it.'* (Because they are asleep to it)

Saying 5- *'Know what is within your sight, and what is hidden from you will become clear to you.'*

Saying 3- *'How long will you sleep?'*

Saying 89- *'You do not know how to study this moment.'*

Pages, 11, 19, 29, 35, 36, 38, 41.

The teaching that we do not know ourselves was left out of the Synoptic Gospels, probably because they did not know what it meant. Here it has a prime spot as it does in much of the ancient literature, Eastern and Greek, before the time of Jesus. The early Church Fathers took this most seriously. Irenaeus, Origen, Ambrose, St. Cyril, and countless others preached and wrote about it.

Just as it is hard to realize that we are in a trance state, drifting through the world as automatons, it is equally difficult to grasp that we are almost completely ignorant of whom we are.

My favorite quote on this subject comes from Socrates. He said, **"Thus in the manner of knowing oneself, the fact that everyone is seen to be so cocksure and self-satisfied**

that everyone thinks he understands enough about himself, signifies that everyone understands nothing about it. *An unexamined life is not worth living.*"

In modern Christian Theology, the idea of Self-Knowledge is treated as a superfluous antique, if it is thought about at all.

We are not these bodies, but rather our psychology, which is invisible. Our outer production is here for all to see. It is what is behind the curtain that is most important and is blacked out except for the most ardent seekers..

We are atomic beings. That is we are made from atoms. But our lives are intangible and obscure, concealed under the folds of motives and stimuli we are only vaguely aware of. We have been trained by life to look out, not in. By studying our thoughts, emotions, and imaginations, quietly and without judgment, we can begin to encounter a whole different creature living inside our perishable bone cages. This then, after years of effort, will open our inner eye so we can become enlightened about the nature of ourselves that is the window to the essence of everything. It is a Divine Mission. The more we know ourselves the closer we become to Immortal Beings.

Chapter 8:1-'*But when the Lord saw that we were sad, he said, "For this reason I tell you this so that you may know your selves.*'

-When you know yourselves, then you will be known and will understand that you are children of the living Father. But if you do not know your selves, then you live in poverty, and embody poverty,'

-'Whoever has come to know the world has discovered a carcass, and whoever has discovered a carcass is worth more than the world.'

-Whoever finds self is worth more than the world.'

-You should not be ignorant about yourself. You will be described as one who knows self. For whoever does not know self does not know anything, but whoever knows self already has acquired knowledge about the depth of the universe.'

Pages, 20, 33, The Sower. These three parables, which are familiar to us all, represent two things for me. First, the idea that Christ's teaching can only be grasped by a few, although many have the opportunity. The Heavenly Host only buys the finest produce. It is very similar to the saying about the gate being narrow and few there are to come through it. Immortality is intentionally made difficult. It must be earned.

I think the religion our Founding Father was introducing was not concerned with how many times we go to church or how much we contribute to the basket. He set up a situation where inner self-improvement was paramount and preached to that part in us that could hear it.

The second thing these Parables tell me is that the prize is worth everything, worth the effort that is required. It is hard to imagine that one pearl is worth all that man's merchandise, but not when you know that the pearl is the key to the Kingdom.

-'He said, 'A person is like a wise fisher who cast a net into the sea, and drew it up from the sea full of little fish. Among them the wise fisher discovered a fine big fish, so he threw all the little fish back into the sea and kept the big fish. Whoever has ears to hear ought to listen.'

-'Jesus said, 'The kingdom of the Father is like a merchant who had a supply of merchandise, and then found a pearl. Now the merchant was smart. He sold the merchandise and bought that single pearl for himself.' 'So it is with you: seek after the treasure that is unfailing, that is abiding.

Pages 23, 31. Christ liked the idea of something so small, so seemingly insignificant, blooming into something momentous and magnanimous. He himself was that. A lowly carpenter's son, born poor in a small insignificant, strife torn land, who rose to become the most honored man and teacher in history. The important part of this first little parable is that the seed was planted on 'prepared ground.' This can be our story if we do the prep work.

'They said to Jesus, 'Tell us what the Kingdom of Heaven is like.' He said, it is like a mustard seed, the tiniest of *all seeds. But when it falls on prepared soil, it grows into a large plant and shelters the birds of the sky.*

Jesus said, 'Show me the stone the builders rejected: that is the cornerstone.'

Jesus said, 'Whoever has something in hand will be given more, and whoever has nothing will be deprived of even the tiny bit that person has.'

Page 26. Jesus gives a number of examples of those that do good by him will be given more and the laggard will be stripped of even the scraps they have.

I tell you the truth: whoever listens to what you have to say and turns away, or sneers, or smirks at these things, will be handed over to the ruler who is on high. They will be imprisoned there and will never escape, for their folly will not be forgiven,'

Pages 46, 47, 48. It does not seem to be the current liberal Christian teachings to consider the possibility of punishment after an ill-advised life, but in these writings and all the Synoptic Gospels it is full with exactly that promise. I personally believe it and guide my life by that possibility.

" *-Woe to you who hope in the flesh, and in the prison that will perish! You base your hope upon the world, and your god is this life. You are destroying your souls! You laugh! You express your delight with foolish laughter! You do not realize* *that you will be destroyed. You do not realize your plight. You do not realize you live in darkness and death.'*

In closing, let me say that the Old Time Religion of every sort, Christian, Mid-Eastern, Far Eastern, and Near Eastern, demanded something different from their followers than today. But then there were no such things as religious wars, pogroms, and the like. It was a personal battle against vanity and pride, violence, greed, and all the other diseases that afflict spiritual mankind. The Gospel of Thomas is a vestige of those olden days of a purer pursuit of everlasting life.

I have a book here with a special poem, a gift, from Persia:

THE WALLED GARDEN OF TRUTH
by Hakim Sanai
12th Century Sufi Poet
How will you ever know Him
As long as you are unable
To Know Yourself.
Knowing what you know,
Be serene also, like a mountain
Become a slave
And you will become a king
Good and evil have no meaning
In the world of the Word.

All mankind is asleep
Turn your face toward the world of life,
And turn your back on rank and reputation
The Way is not far...
You yourself are that Way.

WHAT DO WE MEAN WHEN WE SAY 'I' ?

15 March 2015

"'Then Jesus demanded. 'What is your name?' 'My name is Legion, because there are many of us inside this man.'"   -Mark 5:

What I am about to say is not something we usually think about. You have to go to another place inside yourself to hear this. You probably have not heard anything like it before and would have a hard time finding it written anywhere.

Because it is such a different view of how the mechanics of life work, it won't fit into any popular psychological theory or religious tract. It is separate, and like it says in the Parable 'Do not put new wine in old wineskins,' it won't hold another way of thinking. So, please lay aside for a time—set and settled opinions about how life works and I'll pour you some thought provoking new wine.

*

Everywhere we look in life, from a spider's delicate thread to the mighty bright sun, and all between, are complex entities. All the way up and down the spectrum of the Universe are fantastically organized realms beyond our understanding. Worlds within worlds, like endless Russian nesting dolls, are how the Universe is built. We are dealing with a much higher order of intelligence than we can even conceive. Our mission, should we accept it, is to try to grasp the many levels of this awe-inspiring experience we've somehow found ourselves.

But nothing is more daunting than figuring out the puzzle of our identity.

We are bombarded all day with an avalanche of sensory input coming at us from five intake receptors, swarming the brain with its billion of neurons and trillions of synapses. Somehow all of this activity is instantaneously integrated and becomes our reality. No one knows how, but from it we get a sense of personhood, a separate entity.

However, when we use the word 'I' we never think of what it really means or who is really using the 'I.' We say, I want this, I think this, I am sleepy, I am mad, and so on. If you could think about, it might make you wonder, what am I? Am I my body, my name, my soul, myself, my being? The words, 'I

Am,' is the name of God in the Old Testament, yet we use it without thinking. What is it that uses the name of God?

I realize this is semantics, but not the question of who am I. That is a deep philosophical query that is never dealt with at all because it is too hard to think about. In fact we usually use other phrases to express ownership by this thing we call 'I.' We say, 'My arm, My feelings, My idea, My consciousness,' and so on. What is this 'My' that possesses all those emotions, and thoughts, or even things outside of us, my car, or my dinner?

We each have an idea of who we are based upon the edifice we have constructed. What we want others to think we are, and what we think we are, is our attachments: clothes, cars, jobs, attitudes, companions, or honors. They all make up what we present as our identity, but it is for show only passing as reality. We are peeping and hiding behind all these outward moving parts.

We do not know ourselves, as Socrates would say.

One of the great secrets in our psychological makeup is that, like the quote in Mark's Gospel, there are many people in each person. Man's greatest illusion is that he is one. Even now, on the inside, each person is a throng of people, changing to fit a situation. 'I am angry' is not the same person as 'I am delighted.' Each has different attitudes, vocabulary, and even facial expressions. We can be likened to a ship full of sailors, each with a different job.

Our genes may remain the same, but we <u>are</u> our psychology, not our body. Physically we are grown–up clones of our younger selves. Not so inside. We can have a calm demeanor, seemingly in control, but our interior world is likely a roiling jumble of an ever-changing background.

Or at a higher level there are three minds in one person, analogous to our belief of three persons in one God. They are, the body, the emotions, and the intellect. All require the brain to function, but are quite different in their nature and scope. Each mind is a different level of existence. But within each mind is an array of servants.

The servants go by the name 'I,' and in fact are each an individual 'I', just one of hundreds that circulate within us, silent unless we verbalize them. These are not thoughts per se, but can be. They are real but invisible. They run our body, our emotions and our intellect. We are like one of those rooms filled with mirrors. Everywhere you look you can see a different angle of yourself. But in our case, every angle has a different function and acts as if it is the only view, or 'I.'

Every I in us has a job, but too often certain ignorant or ill-suited I's grab the helm and steer us into places not fitted to our best interests. Each major part of us, the body, emotions, and intellect, have pools of I's to run our lives. The I's of the body, which is the world's most complex chemical factory, are only concerned with living in the physical world in comfort and safety. They say when to feed it, bathe it, and all the rest of the many functions associated with the body. When you are thirsty, an 'I,' whose responsibility to see that you are not thirsty will tell you to go get a drink, and you will. The I fades away after only that brief time. It's mission complete. Addiction to any substance is an imbalance; a take over of the ship by I's heading for the shoals.

The I's associated with the emotions are concerned with people and will stimulate I's to pay, and have attention paid to it by people. When our feelings are hurt or we feel joyful by the actions of another person, I's will take charge of us and express themselves in word and action. These I's live by attention. Attention is emotional food and without it we wither and die.

I can't emphasis enough the role that attention plays in making us human. We are not human because we have a body, that makes us an animal, but because we have emotions, and they are exclusively propelled by and for attention, which is the purest form of energy, so fine it cannot be measured, only felt.

I know you've heard that a child deprived of attention will grow up stunted emotionally. Well, the same thing happens to adults who are ignored or lonely. They shrink inside for lack of attention—that is, life enhancing energy.

The intellectual part of us will generate thoughts, which are its "I's." Ideas and imagination are generated by the intellect. Memories are relics of by-gone days, and one little I about a person we used to know might quickly lead to a whole cavalcade of I's that carry on a one-sided silent monologue with that long-gone person and last for minutes. Idle imagination like this can consume most of our intellectual capital and leave us with a dime-store mind. The intellectual mind also has the duty to give voice to what the others wish to be known.

Though, invisible and indivisible, I's are real, just like a thought, they can make us do things. They, and only they, motor us through life. Real I, like a ship's captain, or Soul, is the great watcher and our spiritual parent.

So, we drag all these I's along wherever we go. They are not heavy. You can fit them all on the head of a pin. But they can be burdensome if they are not doing their right work and interfering in another's realm. A balanced person is one who has their major parts in symmetry, being emotional, thinking, or physical in the right proportion and at the right time. It is a difficult thing for an individual much less the masses. That is why the world is so full of tumult and confusion, ships ramming and getting tangled up with each other.

New circumstances and all kinds of things create I's. Meet a new person and new I's will emerge with that person's name and image attached, and it is likely to always be a part of you. Our psychic life changes from moment to moment because the I's keep rotating from situation to situation as they are stimulated.

*

There is one Real I within each of us, but it is so buried that its appearance is rare. We can access the Real I when we say, with intention and while feeling the body, 'I Am.' For a few seconds and not much more, we can be who we really are, but soon the Presence of "I Am' goes back to sleep and each one of us is run by this crew of little I's that may have agendas not compatible with the whole ship, or person. The wisdom literature of old, including the Gospels, is replete with references of sleeping mankind. This was the meaning.

During the time the Soul awakens the Divine is alive. That is when rare sparkles of light come from within, when we can have experiences and Know we are experiencing them. With Presence, we have the opportunity to invite God into our lives and to bring some semblance of order to our inner chaos.

Every life is composed of a mass of habits, good habits, bad habits, and even destructive habits. Doing the same things like robots and saying the same things like parrots are the I's that run our ship of state while the captain is asleep.

*

Starting about six centuries before Christ the earth was seeded with men who could teach this deep knowledge. Spread over the East, China, India, and the Mediterranean Sea region, these Holy Ones brought an inner spirituality to the planet that it did not possess before. This was the birth of philosophy, the first draught of deep thought, and a more internally directed religion, an escape hatch from our lower natures.

These seers, guru's and teacher's object was to tame and introduce us to the God within—the <u>I AM</u>. They encouraged and modeled techniques like meditation, chanting, praying, silent retreats, and strict codes of behavior. Through these a more real identity could emerge. Identity is an inside job. It is not the slathering on of outer things, but a kind of birth from our depths. The pinnacle of this period was Jesus of Nazareth who brought Man to a transitional period where the curse we seemed to be living under could be removed by the discovery of the God within. I read once that the original word for God in Sanskrit was Day. So, to bring

God into your life using the tool of Presence is to bring in the light of Day.

After Christ, larger and more diverse groups, sects, cults, and full-throated religions formed up around these implanted bulbs of awakening. The whole of the history of the great mystics was toward the discovery and development of the Real I, The Living God within.

*

In summation, what I am saying to you is that we are not what we think we are, but much more and many more. Each I is a separate person representing a wholly different mind, with goals and personalities. In fact, we could not live without this variety that circulates and inhabits the entity called I.

So, if someone asks who are you, you can say with confidence, sometimes I am tired, sometimes I am happy, sometimes I am sad, and so on, and be totally correct in your answer, for thy name is Legion.

OUR TWO WORLDS

23 March 2014

'In him was life, and that life was the light of men.'
'I am the light of the world.'

Gospel of John

What I want to speak about today is a different way to think about the two worlds that we live in, the visible and the invisible. Eventually I want to relate them to the reason we require religion and spirituality in our lives.

By visible I mean generally anything that the five senses can detect by themselves or with high tech aides. Without the senses we would not have a physical reality. Through them are rendered the apparent solidness of our existence. However, it is only through other means, undetectable to the senses, that all of this is possible.

Light is not visible, but it does make many things observable by reflecting off objects, and that is how we can know there is such a phenomena as light. In this case the invisible illuminates the visible. Fortunately, we come with ready-made receptors, eyes that are programmed to receive light and its array of color. Light is the initiator of complex life on earth through photosynthesis. In addition, light is eternal. A star 14 Billion light years away still transmits its rays to us. Not only that, but the star casts its beacon of light in an ever increasing halo. We are bathed in heaven's glow.

Also, this is the same with many other phenomena of nature, like gravity, we can see what it does and even calculate its force, but not gravity itself.

If we made a list of the things in the sensible world it would be short. Bodies and objects are about all we could really list, and at any one time that would be restricted to where we are. We are extremely limited in our scope by the five outer senses. We do have many invisible inner senses that translate those outer ones, like sense of humor, justice, wonder, beauty, and honor.

My grandma used to take me to a grotto at the bottom of a large church in Cincinnati. I can still remember the feel of that place of prayer. Even as a little boy I knew to go to my knees. Candles were lit by people trying to reach God. Compare that with a tour of Alcatraz. It is frightful and ominous, the haunt of evil and torment still ricochet off the walls. Both places emitted an invisible atmosphere no meter would ever detect. What is left behind never leaves.

Scientists can only study what the outer senses deliver, the material world. They can also study incredibly small things like cells and large bodies like stars with the assistance of telescopes and microscopes, and even reach farther down and out by using mathematics. But they run aground when they go beyond the descriptive and try to put qualities to the things they see because they've dipped into the unknown world of the invisible. Quantities are observable. Qualities are not. They are assigned. Things can only live by virtue of the qualities given to them by humans. Material objects are in neutral. Our mind puts them in gear.

*

Whereas the visible is a blip on a screen of the electromagnetic spectrum, the range and depth of the invisible universe is immense. Our physical world wafts through the non-physical world like a feather in the wind.

Our thoughts and emotions are invisible to the spyglasses of science but are integral to our experience of this world. We are all filled with a variety of constantly shifting sentiments and feelings like joy or sorrow that may belie our exterior appearance. They are what motivate us to do things and manipulate objects. This includes harboring opinions and attitudes.

However, our opinions and attitudes are stuck to us like barnacles and everywhere we go we have to lug them around. We can only really <u>think</u> from ideas that use newly minted thoughts. We cannot think from our opinions or attitudes. They are incased in hard silos of crusty old thoughts. We trundle them out and do a pantomime of intelligence. There is, however, a mystic stream of new thoughts coming to us from where we know not, and flying away to parts just as unknown. Our attitudes keep them from landing.

As I said, human interaction of all sorts completely relies on the abstract, love, hate, conscience, ethics, concepts, ideas, illusions, and countless other characteristics. Each of these non-things makes us who we are, regardless of physical features. Great is the dazzle of the paper-thin world, but the genuine article, essence, is invisible to the naked eye.

Our language is rife with metaphors and similes because we don't have words for the invisible motives and drivers of people's behavior. We often describe individual personalities using animal metaphors like a bull in a china shop, a snake in the grass, a peacock, a tiger, a mouse, a chicken, etc. All of these substitutes try to label a person's inner world in terms of the solid outer one.

We live inside bodies, but are not our bodies which rot by the minute.

Beliefs are invisible, but oddly inflexible like steel girders. They trump mere common sense almost every time. Beliefs can propel us into all kinds of destructive and unwise behavior like the handling of poisonous snakes or strapping explosives to oneself as a means to heaven.

People can see the outer environment, but we live in our mind and use these holes in our head to navigate our way around. And we can easily escape into the confines of our imagination. While doing almost anything, driving, walking, and so on, we live silent in our whimsy. We can do and say what we want without repercussions. Life itself is endurable because of imagination. The invisible world we create inside is our principle entertainer and friend for life, and is made up of figments only.

*

Life itself is a most confounding enigma, an indefinable state of being like an electric current. We can't see life, only what it sparks. It is an inner fire. Everyone has a different glow, bright or dull. When we die, the flame is snuffed, leaving a burnt out carcass. There is nothing left to love. At funerals we talk about the light that was.

We have to put Time in this category too. What is time? It is inscrutable. You can't touch or see it, but you need it to do anything or go anywhere. It stretches and shrinks. It is invisible but real.

Consciousness, which is invisible and unknowable, is responsible for why we can speak, think, and act. It is certainly not explainable by any technical measure. Attention is fundamental to consciousness and it resides only in our heads and we are the only ones who can know we are attentive. It is our invisible money in the spiritual/psychological world. We must pay attention for whatever we want.

Cells in our body are part of the visible world if we have the right equipment to see them, but they operate from unseen information and laws that are part of the other world. Each of our trillions of cells is chock full of instructions that are byzantine in complexity. One cell, called a Zygote, can produce the most mind-bending ecosystem, structures and intricate systems within systems. The human body has 60,000 miles of vessels, arteries, and capillaries, and a brain with one hundred billion neurons. And all of this information is coded in that first cell, with its impossibly intricate wiring, braided together and fueled by the unknown life force.

Nature's entire canon is concealed from prying eyes. We can observe the results of the laws, but not the laws themselves and all their perturbations. The Universe is jam packed with invisible laws and all must receive their due. We always can see the end products, the flowers, the mountains, and the animals, but not the mandates from which these things spring because they are shrouded in mystery.

The Empire of the Invisible has vast holdings and contains the unknown. Every time we take a step forward toward the future a little of this ignorance is dispelled but it is just a single baby step in an endless journey. If you think about it, the future is dark, the present is light, and the past is twilight, fading to black. Memory then is yesterday's light, poorly perceived.

*

172

To me atheism is based on the presumption that the only part of the universe that matters or needs to be explained is the material in it. Unbelievers have many theories surrounding about how suns, planets, flora and fauna manifested without the aid and direction of Higher Mind. They point to the incredible fine-tuning of the universe and our planet in terms of chance occurrences. God deniers conveniently set aside any notion of the invisible phenomena that is the engine behind it all.

They believe in life, light, and thought because they experience them and think they exist only by happenstance, and dismiss with distain those who believe in our darling God as the giver of life, light, and thought.

I would agree with the materialists that the world operates as a machine, a stimulus response mechanism. The physical things of the world are on automatic. Our blood courses through our veins, a rose lives and dies, and the earth rolls around on a tight schedule. But what lies behind all of the mechanics is the idea that the invisible, the non-material part of this world, is responsible. It looms in the background and has great influence over the whole of this business. In fact, the material world has no meaning, no purpose, without the corresponding immaterial world.

We do not know where thoughts come from, or how deep are the emotions we might have in the next moment.

Yet, they push us around where they may. We have no idea of what comes next from just around the corner.

*

There is no food like love. What a healer! It is a salve against all things bad. There is also no enemy like hate and all the rest of the devils, envy, jealousy, spite, and so on. Our only protection from those dark ones is by our good angels, kindness, thoughtfulness, decency, and love.

Every group of people, ancient or modern, have felt the invisible force within them and developed many strategies to deal with it, using religious objects, rituals and sometimes outlandish beliefs to pay homage to the unseen, but powerfully felt force of life.

The birth of humanity is also the birth of awe. Curiosity of what and how has marched together with overwhelming emotions at the spirit behind the vistas and enchantment of life itself. Reverence and adoration became the response. Religion was born of this high stuff.

With religions we have always had visible objects like prayer books, chalices, and other materials and symbols. But they are there only because they represent or remind us of the invisible sacred phenomena, God, angels, souls, heaven, hell, grace, and so on. Those lucky ones, those who have discovered Religion and its quiet satisfactions, plead their case and venerate what they do not exactly understand but have pure Faith in, the cloaked Realm of God. They have made a holy connection to the invisible.

*

Know this above all: *God is Light!* God's fiery generator is our Sun whose influence is absolute. We can't look or approach it as it streams invisible energy down from above, a radiating beam of love. The sun's comings and goings are perpetually in a blaze of glory. It is God's rays that warm everyone without judgment, and enlightens all those who wish it.

There is one God with many Suns. You can see them any night by lifting your eyes heavenward. By opening the shutters of your mind, God will be with you always and in all ways.

God's great gift to us is the opportunity to be able to partake of the Light. That is what religion is all about, the seeking of Light, a treasure without end.

CATERPILLAR COATS

2 February 2014

I wanted to take a little time to talk about today's Gospel reading, especially the first sentence, to wit:

"You are the salt of the earth; but if salt has lost its taste, how can its saltiness be restored? It is no longer good for anything, but is thrown out and trampled underfoot.

This sentence does not belong with the rest of the reading. In fact, there are at least three different ideas shoved into the one paragraph. I've noticed this in other places in the Gospels. There is some cut and paste activity going on here, but all of the ideas are from Higher School. They are just a bit scrambled.

The above quoted passage is an analogy that relates salt to a person with an active vibrant soul, and one whose soul is dead, just a shell, a sort of spiritual zombie. There is no such thing as salt losing its saltiness, but souls can go lifeless and limp.

This passage more belongs a few chapters later where Christ says to let the dead bury the dead. In other words, heaven has no use for people who do not have Faith, Faith that keeps them alive inside. This means those who do not try to understand their spiritual nature, that do not attempt crack the code of the sacred, and who have no quest beyond the temporal. That is what he meant by loss of saltiness. They are no longer good for anything to the Celestial world and they will be trampled underfoot.

Jesus was a very serious man. He did not kid around. He made us work to grasp the meaning behind his Teaching. Taken literally, his examples do not make much sense. As metaphors, as allegories, as analogies, they rise to heaven's very gate.

As our level rises, so the meanings of Christ's words emerge from their literal hiding place. I believe the key to this is the development of an ever-increasing level of appreciation of creation, our universe radiant with intelligence and teeming with wonders without end.

As I grasp it, about 14 Billion years ago there was a remarkable event. It was the first event ever. It was not a Bang, but a GRAND ILLUMINATION. Suddenly light! Great and many balls of flame were hurled on a far path from this powerful source, producing space and time on the fly. Each started a complex chemical process that would eventually lead to the CROWNING ACHIEVEMENT of Greater Mind—human beings.

But, here we have Jesus saying in effect that when we, as special envoys and creations, are no longer alive, no longer moved by this strange land with its cornucopia of enchantments: from the delicate butterfly to the waterlogged hippopotamus, and rainbows to warthogs, we no longer really exist as God's special creatures. We become stick people. We can still carry out our assigned roles in the machinery of life, but we lose our place in God's immense moral universe.

We were not cast initially in this concrete mold but given a lively essence to develop. But too often life's humdrum wears us down with the same dull thoughts, attitudes, opinions, and prejudices, and never allows us to shake free and out of our small boxy minds.

Those that do not make efforts to bloom and bear fruit, lose their saltiness, their real life. They become walking, talking shadows, echoes only.

If, on the other hand, the soul awakens, looks around and cries, "I want to live!" That then is a reenactment of the return of the Prodigal Son and our own personal resurrection.

Have you ever seen a caterpillar? They are ugly and ungainly, little freaks of Nature. And yet, under the right circumstances she can become Nature's most beautiful prize and lift off to the heavens. So, we too can break from our caterpillar coats and waft upwards.

WHY WE ARE HERE

24 February 2013

From an early age I was seduced by the eternal world of ideas. Philosophy enticed me and made me seek a life of the Mind, hostile to ignorance and a friend to knowledge. I like to pluck a juicy subject, peel the rind, and ponder its interior secrets from different angles.

The one puzzle that stimulates me more than any other is the question of why humans are here at all? What is the meaning of our existence? I never hear it from the pulpit or in any discussions anywhere. I don't think anyone wants to think about it. We may be afraid of the answer.

If you are of the school of thought that the Universe, the earth and all its creatures are the result of a vast array of near impossible fortunate flukes, fine-tuned by sheer chance, then the question of why we are here would never arise. But if, like me, you consider that we live in a universe that burst into existence full of purpose and meaning, then the query carries value.

This is why I set my goal early to meditate on it. I know there are deep, hidden processes, <u>laws</u>, at work beyond our imaginings. To find them I had to begin by looking from a different angle. It is too easy to be fooled otherwise.

I began by studying the Bible from another perspective, especially Genesis. I concluded that the stories were not true as such, but rather the 'Truth.' They spell out the nature of the people that God created, not their history. These are allegories that are as poignant and as pinpoint today as they were thousands of years ago. Man is a caustic and wearisome creature and <u>designed</u> to be that way.

As the story goes, the first two put on this planet, Eve and Adam, had everything they could ever want and yet yearned for more and defied even God to have it. Then the first child born, Cain, turned into a murderer. God did not punish him but sent him away. God protected him from harm. Cain later prospered and became the progenitor of a race of people. In other words, the good man was disabled and his killer was sent out to raise more Cain. Thus, it seems we have come down from a lumbering foul savage.

Genesis goes on and shows God angry with his people. It says in Chapter 6, verse 11, *"Now the earth was corrupt in God's sight and was full of violence."*

So, God flooded the world and hurled fire bolts on errant cities. But even afterwards, the allegories keep pouring forth in the same manner for 11 chapters, a stubborn, mean spirited people going about their merry way.

That is how humanity began according to Scripture. And the world has not abated its hard ways since that time, but instead polished and sharpened them. One writer called Genesis '*a highly condensed version of the tragic nature of human history.*' The blood of Cain runs through us all.

If we could <u>look</u> down on earth God seems to have created mankind as perpetually strutting and preening, or bemoaning and bewailing their lot in life, being stuffed together like absurd monkeys in a cage.

However, <u>looking</u> from here, the history of the world is sad, one of crime, violence and greed, causing all manner of distress. Even more to the point, the earth is a place of suffering, as the Buddha said, but most of it is at the hands of each other. There is plenty of hardship just living on this grumpy earth without mankind's adding the wrath of rogues and rascals waving war clubs. Without a doubt, war is perpetual because it provides suffering and suffering is part of our lot.

Yet, at the same time, shining examples can immerge from the heap that proves we do not all have to be wild brutes or buffoons on earth. There are many examples of the good peeping through the muck of dark deeds like a lighted citadel. God has given us great leeway in how we act, for good or ill.

We can escape the downward grind and resurrect Able and let him live in us again.

*

Mother Earth is a giant <u>living</u>, rotund queen with a white crown, swooping in grand orbits around Old Man Sol. It is enfolded in a soft protective, gauze-like atmosphere, with a beating heart at her core, and a furry and moist outer skin, dining through immense induction vents and then expelling her waste through volcanoes and undersea crevasses, thus producing a nutrient rich soil for the growth and maintenance of flora and fauna. It is all quite wonderful and miraculous.

Amid all this beauty and mystery sits mankind on a stately throne, the crowning achievement of the whole enterprise of creation, Father God and Mother Earth's pampered darlings. But man is also heir to a hefty amount of conflict and torment as part of our legacy. This is <u>payment</u> for all that we have and receive. We, as individuals and as a species are not supposed to be without aches and agonies. Invisible cords bind us to the whipping post. Our psychological design assures it.

The gospels, in various places, seem to agree. One of the important aims of Christ was to generate conflict and the emotions it produces. In Matthew, Chapter 10, Christ says, *"Think not that I came to send peace on the earth. I came not to send peace, but a sword."* Christianity, in its many forms,

182

along with its many blessings and opportunities, certainly has brought grief and sacrifice too many.

But, setting aside our inheritance from Cain and his brood, where our weaknesses and foibles produce disarray and disappointment, individual humans can generate the most unexpected and delightful things, events, and novelties.

In this vein, we can be understood as chemical factories producing a variety of products. We generate energy, consciousness, and ideas. We are endowed with interests and intelligence to study and learn, and creativity to beget artistic delights. We use hands to build interesting structures around us, and hearts to love it all.

*

But our chemistry, especially in the male half of the species, guarantees mayhem at regular intervals. Inborn with a fury, the doltish male is sated only by war and such other horrors. However, conflict of multiple kinds abounds at every level with both sexes, its woe fully intended.

Why is this, we wonder? The answer is that all ledgers must be balanced. For every debit there is a credit. It is a universal law. We are given so much and so much is taken. No crime goes unpunished. No effort goes unrewarded. Justice will prevail, if not here, then in the next world. '*Every hair is counted,*' said Jesus.

A powerful force of resistance attends all our enterprises, making any progress fraught with problems and complications, but an ancient law, the *Law of Payment* makes progress possible. All humanity is being managed by the Divine Presence. Payments are being extracted from all of us for things we have received or will receive. No free lunch. Payment can be stretched over time or collected before or after an event. It can be hoisted by one person or spread over a multitude. We are always paying or collecting, but without knowing the price tag.

The Jews are God's chosen people, the bible tells us. They have, without a doubt, contributed an immense treasure to humanity over the generations. Everywhere they have settled, like leaven, they have raised the culture to maturity and been a boon to all. The greatest man who ever lived was from that race of giants. Yet, as a group, the Jews have had staggering sufferings, spit upon, harried and murdered wherever they have wandered. Envy has stalked them almost non-stop. The propensity to bully Jews is a common vice. Their lot is one of high suffering for high gifts.

This is not how we suppose life should go logically, but the *Law of Payment* is more sophisticated than we can comprehend. For instance, Jesus delivered an unparalleled message to us from another world, and yet was tortured and murdered for it. Justice for this outrage was delivered offstage.

Many have carried forth with Christ's work and paid dearly for each conversion and church built in his honor.

*

The Universe is a shimmering swarm of energy. Humans are a bottled form of that energy. This energy is what we use to live our lives with, but gets transfigured into useable forms by God for a variety of purposes.

The kind of energy produced by suffering and emotional pain is a psychological or spiritual payment for things we need or have done. We pay to receive our benefits and foot the bill for our misdeeds. On the other hand, negative emotions like spite, bitterness, complaining, worrying, or being hurtful to others is harvested for things of God's choosing. Nothing is wasted.

Think for a moment. If we can look from another angle, our hardships are the nutriments for new things and events. Painful changes produce beneficial situations. Examples are rife in history. The Black Death, with its untold suffering, produced in its wake the end to the inhumane system of serfdom. Likewise, World War I sounded the death knell to the European aristocracy, and our Civil War bought the end of slavery, and so on. The March of history is the clip-clop of payment for improvement. The wrinkles of old age are the price of the bloom of youth.

I am sure each of us can recite many examples of the same phenomena in our own lives, periods of torment like divorce or loss of jobs, actually turning out to be for the best. Think of those misfortunes as veiled fortunes.

Whatever we wish it must be paid for from our stash of whatever we can offer, effort, suffering, or even cash on the barrelhead. God is the paymaster and is no cheapskate, giving full value for top producers.

The devil, on the other hand, is a bottom feeder. His lures promise gain without pain, but it is a trick. He flatters our vanity to watch us flail in our misfortune.

*

Looking at living Nature we can see a recurring pattern. Virtually every creature is the result of many possibilities. During mating of animals millions of seeds pour forth but usually only one becomes a baby, whether by happenchance or some unknown design. An oak tree will drop around fifty thousand acorns in its lifetime and hopefully one or two will end up a full-grown adult tree, the rest becomes food or fertilizer.

In the spiritual world this is the case *also.* Jesus says in Matthew, *"Many* are called, few are chosen." This is what he means. Perhaps only one individual <u>may</u> be chosen, even though whole congregations are called. There are many parables in the Gospels pointing to the difficulty of finding salvation. He never says it is easy because heaven has to be paid for and most ignore the bill pretending no such thing exists. Unless we strive to render to God in the coin of His realm, effort and carrying one's own cross, it won't happen. What I am postulating is not only a loving God, but a business-

186

like God who requires payment for the goods. Every fig tree must produce fruit, or else.

God has created a rich and lavish planet and we are welcome to all her largess, but it is also a proving ground for a future life. The chosen must learn to see from a different angle, as in the opening story. Many walk the path. Most see nothing extraordinary. A few see nothing but.

Know this above all, as Christians, we are the called, not the chosen. It is <u>our business</u> to be chosen.

*

I know this is a difficult thing I bring you. We want, from our churches, an uplifting message and a fellowship that is soothing. We want to know that God's forgiveness is a warm blanket that covers all our misdeeds with His Grace. But it is not so.

We have been given, by the grace of God, not an easy road to the Kingdom, but the opportunity to earn something more profound than words can utter. <u>This is why we are here on earth.</u>

IMAGINARY MYSTICS

27 February 2011

I have a question I am trying to answer. I see in history these so-called mystics who have visions, or for some reason have impressed the masses of their acts of holiness, like the Dali Lama who draws big adoring crowds wherever he goes, or the Pope whose every word is recorded and people swoon when he appears in the window at St. Peters. And then I don't wonder why Jesus called us sheep when I see how the likeness of the Virgin Mary on a taco shell will bring a flock of people to worship in front of it.

There are so many examples of such things in our history that I wonder how to know what is what. A Lama is chosen as a child and trained in the arts and acts of holiness. A Pope is elected to his august position in a highly political conclave. Some arrive with fanfare from the East like Mukanada. Others can transfix the masses with verbose oratory skills. People of all sorts have claimed to be the recipients of messages and visions from above and gathered followers around them. There is virtually no New Age guru who doesn't assert that they have received instructions from on high in a variety of unique ways, some quite laughable. Humanity is easily cast under the spell of celebrity, even religious celebrity, that has its own pomp, costumes, and solemnity, making us starry eyed and agog. We can't know anything about these people's inner life, only the bang and bangle of their parade. " ...*the outward shows be least themselves, the world is still deceived by ornament.*" - Shakespeare

My question is—can a regular person who works on themselves sincerely and unobtrusively for decades, but who never had a mystical experience of any sort, reach the Promise Land? And should one bow and scrape to those few who say they do? Maybe we should be careful not to throw the keys of our Soul to dwarfs and gnomes—quacks that look like swans.

Can those monks who trail the Dali Lama around holding his garment, be actually way ahead of their master in Being and consciousness? Can a simple nun working in a school in some remote village in India, be more sanctified than Mother Teresa who traipsed the world to acclaim and renown? Does one need to be an icon of religion to receive heavenly applause?

Oh, I hope not. I am old school, or old church, who is betting my life that among the flock can emerge one who escapes terrestrial notice, but not celestial notice. To me that is what religion is about, coaxing the chosen one or few out of the many. It is not the getup that goes to heaven, it is those who get up and work.

Actually, where I come from it is taught that our lives are all arranged. We are given a certain mentality, tendencies and talents, circumstances of family and a stream of experiences that carefully mold us. All of this is preparation to carry out our role in life on this our globe theater. We each get to play ourselves in this production, but we can't up and quit.

When we go to make decisions, the weight of all this forces us into the narrow lane of activity. We are each experiments or pilot programs in salvation. We have more restrictions than leeway. We are pulled like magnates along a story line. If we accept this, and not take credit or assign blame for what happens, life can be a great show.

The idea that we live in a kind of play is much older than Shakespeare's immortal words. It is one of the most ancient teachings, back to at least the early Indian Veda's.

But what no God can dictate is our inner life while we go through our outer scenes. Whatever inner mountains we move are our own doing. Whatever is ours inside is our harvest. God's agent, Nature, takes the rest. Dust to dust.

So, we each have an assigned part to play, a role that inhabits us. Our outer choices are nil. Our inner ones are many. Whether the Pope's internal world matches the dash and display in his <u>physical</u> world, is his <u>metaphysical</u> work, and we will never see it. We need not be blinded by his earthly splendor.

No doubt some of these honored ones can elevate themselves into higher plateaus, but it can't be because they were picked as a youngster by a clairvoyant to be the <u>Avatar of the Age</u> as Krisnamurti was, or promoted as a Cardinal is. It has to be because of their own efforts aside from their role. And at the same time, no role is so obscure that it can't be made glorious by goodness. Jesus was a lowly tradesman from a backwater district called Galilee who made the most of his opportunities.   It is taught that we can't change our role in life, but we can change how we play it. God's great gift to all is the opportunity to do so. We are children of clay. Our Souls belong to another world and can be heirs to immortality. Whether our Souls are a well-tended and fertile field or a tangle of briars and thorns is our call alone. We can be angel food or devil's food.

*

No one has been told why we are here on earth. Everything on earth is used for something. What is our use?

Jesus has said a few of us are to be reborn into a higher world. Is the world then a filter so only the pure in heart can slip through those narrow gates? What about the rest? Are we fodder, or compost, or crop? Is the earth then only a pain factory producing some secret commodity?

It may be so. The Gospels make it clear that Heaven means business. Matthew, Mark and Luke are written more like warnings labels than stamps of approval. I think Christianity is the only religion that sounds the alarm about our meager prospects, although Christians usually push aside such notions. The world is a pitiless and prickly place. Even the Son of God didn't have it easy in his visit. They marched him to the gallows.

The bulk of the world seems content to grapple over the scraps of recognition and wealth, and leave the notion of heaven to the weak and worried. But the great teachings say we either nurture our spiritual chrysalis or it will wither.

Ladies and gentlemen, we have been blessed with these lives of promise and the time to discover and cherish our Divine Nature. We came well stocked with everything we need for a productive life in the service of the Lord. We are like light bulbs. We got plugged into this huge system and the light came on at birth illuminating a world full of miracles. But we can be the best of all miracles, for we can sprout our wings again and fly back up to heaven, where we began.

THE EMOTIONAL MIND

4 September 2011

I've thought deeply about how to present these next comments of my offering today because it is an example of Metanoia, thinking in a different way. New ideas can have great transforming power, but also they can be hard to hear at first. There are no grooves ready to receive them in our consciousness. But we need fresh concepts in religion that we can <u>see</u> with the mind's eye. Now mostly our views are vague abstractions like peering into a mist. We talk and think past each other. With that is mind here is a new idea.

*

We have two things that distinguish us from those hairy monsters that live in the trees and eat bananas. One is an Intellectual Mind and the other is an Emotional Mind. There is another Mind called the Instinctive Mind that governs the physical and mechanical functions of the body, like digestion and our carnal drives. The three Minds make up one complicated machine that is the human being. None of these departments are under our direct control; thoughts come unbidden, feelings percolate up, and the blood runs without our slightest notice. The parts, or Minds, do interact in complex ways but are quite apart and also independent of each other at times.

Today I'd like to say a few words about the Emotional Mind. I am not speaking about the brain, which is an earthly organ and part of the Instinctive Mind.

The Emotional Mind is a separate entity that was implanted in these specially designed animals we walk around in. It is like a pod that opens up and is full of interesting equipment. There are different levels producing different kinds of emotion, depending on the situation. There is a lower level for the commerce of everyday life, necessarily shallow. There is a middle level for more intense and demonstrative emotions, often unstable. Finally there is encapsulated at the very pinnacle of our Being a more precious part that is the module that can separate and wing us to heaven. It is sibling to the Soul. Its emotions, like appreciation, gratitude, compassion, and love, sits atop our lives like encrusted jewels. It is the spirit that lives within.

The Emotional Mind, and especially the top tier, is why the call of religion is so insistent in the human. It wishes to waft up and away from this hard earth. In response we are constantly calling home with our prayers and going to church hoping to hear news of our Father's House.

I try to stimulate the higher part of the Emotional Mind with story and poetry that I read. The Emotional Mind communicates through images or pictures. So, stories, which are moving pictures, are vital to human society. We tell each other stories almost non-stop, and in effect, create images to live by. I say we don't know another person until we know their story.

Science cannot understand the Emotional Mind. It is a greater order of reality. It has structure, but it is a psychological construct and cannot be measured, only felt. Its effects can be seen but not its source, which is veiled. We feel many of our strongest emotions in the solar plexus because we have sensors on the inside of the chest that is stimulated when we are emotional. That is why we call it our heart. It is so poetic. It contains the lyrics of our longing. ("*So teach us Lord, to count our days that we may gain a wise heart.*" Psalm 89)

The Emotional Mind gives us a rich, colorful existence and contains both heaven and hell. We can wallow in low, sinister emotions like envy, hate, and anger, or fly with the cherubs in kindness, thanksgiving, or love.

Its only areas of concern are the human and spiritual realms. Therefore, communities, families, all kinds of institutions, and churches with their various ceremonies depend on emotion to keep our life moving and provocative. With its vast stores of energy, the Emotional Mind provides the power for living in society, to reap the joys and sorrows of our social world. Our gossip, our charity, our guilt, our gentleness, and even the dark arts of violence and hate, are all fueled by emotional energy, channeled down different pipes.

*

Everyone has differently developed parts of the Emotional Mind. There are even some who deride emotion as a weakness. It is not a frailty at all, but is an important tool in the conduct of a balanced life. People who accuse others of being 'too emotional' are themselves often overdeveloped in other areas of their being and miss out on the rewards of an interesting life, which only emotion can provide. Some of these are hard-hearted and can be mean without remorse. They have been denied empathy and benevolence in their kit of life skills.

The Emotional Mind is unbelievably tender and sensitive. Many men would risk their physical body in a wide variety of crazy enterprises, like doing back-flips on a motorcycle or tromping off to war without a care as to the consequences, but don't ever hurt their feelings or they will become mush or raving idiots bent on destruction. A 'Dear John' letter will destroy the bravest of us. We couple with bodies, but we love with our whole heart.

*

The Emotional Brain must eat. Its food is called impressions. That is data coming in through the five senses. The really high, nutritious food for the soul are impressions like great art, a Rembrandt self-portrait, a Bach Cantata, a

Shakespeare sonnet, or a quiet church, or the smile of a sweet friend. They can feed us for the better and be lunch for the journey upward.

We still need roughage, the jarring impressions that life sends our way whether we like it or not, the disappointments, the heartaches, the news of tragedy are but ballast to keep us balanced. Impressions like this can make us flounder, but somehow we do learn to swim past the danger and hurt, and become better swimmers in the process.

But too many harsh and violent impressions, if we invite them into us intentionally, as in horror novels or violent movies, will have us walking around like spiritual dwarfs.

*

I just wanted to take these few minutes to acquaint you in a general way with an idea that is ageless, but mostly unknown in the modern world. The idea of the Emotional Mind can never become popular because popularity itself is a poison that will dilute and destroy it. Soon, experts would emerge and arguments would ensue and it would go the way of all truth, torn apart and scattered.

KNOW THYSELF

18 March 2012

'When you know your Self, then you will be known. But if you do not know your Self, then you will live in poverty.' -Jesus,
Gospel of Thomas

''He who knows himself knows the Lord."

-Muhammad

'He who know others is learned. He who knows his Self is wise.'

-Lao-Tzu

'If a man holds himself dear, let him Watch his Self carefully.'

-Buddha

There is one sure but difficult road to enlightenment as taught by the esoteric teachings of the world, including Christianity, Buddhism, and Hinduism. This is not a system of ceremonial worship as spelled out by different religions, which are mainly about how to act in community.   Rituals satisfy some primal need in people to belong to something higher than themselves. Countless temporal leaders have met this need with special doctrines and language as glue to hold their flock together. Only a few real avatars, Jesus, Buddha, Plato and some other ethereal ones, taught internal and external lessons. They broke from the herd and championed a purely individual approach. The Way they taught toward enlightenment is personal and psychological. It is by way of self-knowledge, or as it is said, to Know Thy Self.

This may seem incomprehensible to the average Christian who believes that by going to church on Sunday's is the ticket to ride. However, the deeper teachings of our founders stressed was using one's own life seven days a week as the main spiritual classroom.

To modern religion's spokesmen self-study is only a peripheral concern and rarely mentioned. Yet, life is a hopeless tangle, a knitter's nightmare. Churches are clueless on how to unravel the knot. The Way up and out is through self-study. But few know what it is or what it really means to Know Thyself. Everyone thinks they do of course, and this keeps people from pursuing this knowledge. Who would seek something they already have?

Of course, this is far from the case. Our psychological makeup is a deep secret and virtually no one is allowed in the vaults of their selves. The modes and roads to the Self have been lost. It is a forgotten art.

*

This is what I would like to talk about today. You may not get another chance to encounter this idea. It has been shunted aside by the modern world as undecipherable and a trifle of negligible importance.

Much of what I will say here today has been said before. I'm just bunching it up for you so you don't have to read 100 obtuse volumes. The once clear path to self-knowledge that the ancients trudged is now buried under an avalanche of distractions. There are too many bouncing baubles that bewilder us to make self-study the focus and object of one's living. Self-study means to concentrate on one's inner world.

Life provides the raw material for self-study. Our reactions and thoughts are what are studied. Every situation we encounter can give us impersonal knowledge of ourselves, not the personal and highly biased opinions as is usual. In this endeavor just to see what we do and how we think is the goal. Then who we really are will slowly emerge. The negative or positive judgment of ourselves and our actions has no place in self-study. There is one thing for sure that can be discovered. We are nothing like we suppose, but we have to uncover this for ourselves. Self-knowledge must well up from inside. The more we view ourselves as interesting strangers the clearer we can see our foibles and proclivities.

*

In order to begin I will give you a primer on how the inner world, our psychology, is constructed. We can easily see that the outer world, our bodies, has an intricate system to them as part of the animal kingdom. That tiny seed in the womb is programmed to produce a completely functioning human animal, a complex chemistry and erector set with trillions of interlocking parts.

Our spirituality also has intelligence behind the design as an important addendum to Mother Nature's masterpiece. When we are conceived the Gods plant a spiritual seed into the sprouting organism. This embryo is called Soul or Self. It is our Divine infant voice too faint to be heard yet. We can never see it. We must experience it. This is our individual Essence marking us as unique from all other beings in the Universe. In it is enfolded all of our innate potential not connected to our animalistic natures. This seedling is designed to evolve into an angel.

Not long after birth a child begins to develop a personality to be a touchstone to the outside world. This is supposed to be a clear covering that allows our Essence to grow. However, not long after personality begins to form, darkness descends on the young soul, cutting out the light with a pseudo personality. This false personality is what we are definitely not and stunts the Soul's growth. It forms in response to the blending with society that model how to act, not how to be. We become a creature of those around us. Think of the Soul as a piece of gold in a jar. The false is a stiff and opaque coating that hides its radiance.

By the time a child is three or four, he or she has developed a host of counterfeit acts designed to protect itself and get what it wants. Gradually the innocence and raw potential of our Spirit is smothered in this fabricated covering. The child grows to be an adult and the fiction is compounded chiefly through the imitation of those around us. All kinds of situations give rise to different versions of ourselves, none of which reflect our Soul. Each version is a marionette pulled by an assortment of strings—ambitions, popularity, fear, and so on.

The cranks and wheels of outer life drive us away from the truth. Soon, we are fooled by our own pretense. We become caricatures of real people. A two year old is more real than a 40 year old because a child has not been fully civilized yet. His or her innocence is still astir. Lying is a staple of a functioning society and has many uses, some of which are quite beneficial. Children are gradually introduced to our world of prevarication. As a result of socialization, we have a whole world of walking hoaxes and nothing is what it pretends to be. We are more a big soufflé—shadows, echoes.

This is our illusionary world built haphazardly on a false premise. We are not one personality, but a conglomeration of persons thrown together, not for better, for worse. And that begets a skewed relationship with our selves. We believe our own façade. Priorities become confused and important things are passed over for a dash and dab of the superficial.

Our God given Soul or Essence is mostly buried or comes out in distortion. However, for an individual this does not have to be. If he or she would start a lifelong program of self-examination it will lead bit by bit to self-knowledge, the lost country of our Essence. As Socrates said, "*An unexamined life is not worth living.*"

To live in a counterfeit world and to develop artificially is quite natural on earth, but the goal that Christ, Socrates, and a host of other blessed ones propose is a supernatural one. We, short-lived beings, built up out of dust, are thrown into a game of charades to puzzle out before we blow away.

The aim here is to peel back the false fabric by the power of observation. Much of the fraudulent will evaporate as it comes to light. To tease apart the false from the true, the false personality from the Essence, is to discover the Self. The aim here is not to create a perfect person, but rather a person who understands themselves without their many masks. The mature part of a person is their understanding, not their show. The Soul remains forever young but gets slathered with theatrical make-up as the years go by.

As the Soul's nemesis, false personality, begins to atrophy, we will see how much we have been deluded all these years. Our worst enemy is the person we thought we were.

Human society is set up to promote illusions and it gives us a kind of cohesion against the uncertainty that surrounds us. They are the stuff of our opinions and the more people share the same opinions the safer we feel. We do love our illusions, but we can't take them with us when we die any more than we can our money. Heaven is an illusion free zone. But do not be mistaken—illusions are real, real in the fact that they make us think and act in certain ways. We make love and war under their sway. Our job is to see our own illusions, which are destructive enough, never mind the world's fancied notions.

So, how does one begin this process of learning about themselves? It is no fun because we have to expose so much ingrained ignorance. We are like a blind man imagining he can see because he has a cane.

Start by watching your thoughts, attitudes, imaginings, prejudices, fears, and resentments, both roaring and subtle. All of this goes on unnoted in each of us because we are not used to keeping a keen eye on our interior parts. Instead of looking dispassionately at ourselves we remain passionately and willfully blind.

Observe, if you can, what you say internally while in differing moods and states, like anger, delight, or whimsy. Each state is a different theater we bring up and become a whole other character to match the mood. Watch what your body does. Every character has distinct facial expressions, tone of voice, and body language to match the new show.

The body is a thing, a beautiful contraption. It surrounds the Soul but belongs to the Soul and is its reason for being. The gods went to a great deal of trouble to create these pockets for the Spirit, but they are still only disposable containers with expiration dates. We are our Soul, not our body. We feed our body, clothe it, take it for a walk, and so on. When we speak we understand this at a visceral level as we say my hand, my head, and my body. Our Soul is the immortal landlord in a mortal casing.

It is the power of self-observation that can free us of the body and its attendant personality. By beginning to observe from a neutral place what we do and what we think is the mighty implement to self-knowledge. It is God's own stain remover.

The nature of our living is against the acquisition of inner knowledge and will fight self-study by bombarding us with diversions to keep us focused on the outside world and apart from any insights we might have. How can we hear the call of destiny with all the racket of life confounding us?

One day you may encounter a small child and have the feeling that it is you from an earlier, innocent time. This child has been born again in you, emerging from all that you were not. Christ said, *"Unless you become as a little child..."*

*

The people I quoted earlier and the many others who have already internalized this message wish to lift you up off your rusty moorings and sail away with them to a far shore. Then our secret wild yearnings for a bolder life will come to fruition and we can begin to live fully in the aura of another world's presence—our own Divine Soul.

The time to begin is now. To reach the Promise Land we must journey through today. Therefore go as far as you can today. Do not waste it. It is full of opportunity.

And finally, this from William Wordsworth, a man who used to live in my bookstore in Los Angeles, on discovering his Soul:

And I have felt
A presence that disturbs me with the joy
Of elevated thoughts; a sense sublime
Of something far more deeply interfused,
Whose dwelling is the light of setting suns,
And the round ocean and the living air,
And the blue sky, and in the mind of man;
A motion and a spirit, that impels
All thinking things, all objects of all thought,
And rolls through all things.

THE HOLY LAND

15 January 2012

On Christmas Eve, 1968, astronauts from the Apollo Eight Mission rounded the moon and came upon the first look at the earth from far away. It was a floating vision of blue and swirling white light against an ink black background. Compared to the moon, which appeared like a chewed up old bone, the planet Earth was a throbbing living membrane, a rolling ball, friendly and inviting with a jaunty white cap. To a stunned TV audience, Jim Lovell read the following words from Genesis: *"In the beginning, God created the heavens and the Earth..."* Frank Borman, six months later on Apollo Eleven, remarked when he saw this same lyrical specter, *"The earth from here is a grand oasis in the big vastness of space."*

*

The earth <u>is</u> truly a miraculous place. Yet, there are those who diminish its value. Carl Sagan, the man who popularized cosmology, rejected its uniqueness and maintained that there are many such places in our own Milky Way. In fact, some Probability Theorists claim that there is millions of life bearing planets throughout the cosmos. Of course, their baseline assumptions are constructed of feathers and sand. There is no way to know such things. The actual probability of the conditions necessary for complex life is impossible to calculate.

Daniel Dennett, an atheist of some note, thinks the whole earth and life itself just popped up out of nowhere, the lucky recipient of countless 'accidents.'

There are others of his tribe who make headlines insisting with an air of certainty that our universe is only one of many universes. This multi-universe hypothesis was already well imagined in the Star Trek TV series and countless science fiction novels. However, other than childish make-believe, there are again no actual facts to back up such statements. The notoriety of these notions is the result of our reliance on authority figures and paper credentials, not any course of reality.

*

So, while this is true and obvious that we are here on this spectacular earth with all the trimmings, we know nothing from physical evidence of <u>why</u> we are here. In fact, Richard Dawkins of Oxford has been telling people for many years that we have no purpose here on earth, no reason for being. He maintains that all these great cycles and rhythms and complexity that permeate the earth are here by chance. Science, he says, has eliminated the need for our standard Creation Myth in Genesis.

True enough, science has made great leaps forward, but while the current popular science periodicals are full of studies and theories on the one hand, they also elucidate the countless puzzles that still remains and are multiplying daily. I read that in 2010 one Biochemical journal was inundated with 197,000 pages of submissions. It seems that the more is known about the general makeup of the cosmos at any level, the more staggering the mystery and the more swallowed by the unknown we become. We drift farther afield in our presumptions the more we find out.

*

The most astonishing aspect of the earth is its people. There are no two humans alike under the skin. Each has a different personality, talents, drives, and general peculiarities. Everyone is a new idea and an ingenious experiment on the grounds of this laboratory. We are spirits installed in bodies, given <u>special powers</u> to taste a strawberry, smell a gardenia, feel a silk scarf, hear a symphony, see a rainbow, and finally, the power and reason to say thank you. We are bathed in a stream of Loving Thought, the product of an artistic vision that transcends the assemblage of genetic material.

*

We cannot begin to fathom the deep intelligence that went into the conceiving and making of our world and the multiple aims it fulfills. We are not here for one purpose, but many. The one we religious folk know about is that a <u>few</u> of us are destined by our <u>own efforts</u> to rise to a Higher Plane, called by our religion Heaven, by others Consciousness, Enlightenment, Nirvana, or the Happy Hunting Grounds. Christ warned us that this was a formidable task to accomplish.

For a reason not clear, but obvious from all the evidence, humanity has to suffer. We are engineered to create a certain amount of affliction for each other. Somehow the negative emotional energy that it generates is used for unknown purposes. For our part, emotions give us a rich, varied life, from heavenly to hellish, and keep life bubbling along. Our emotional makeup is no accident as Daniel Dennett might postulate. It is very well planned and the energy is used by Higher Forces. Our emotional part is a furnace installed to produce power. It is a cooker of high-test energy, like the sun cooks elements to produce carbon.

We all pass through lives filled with various kinds and levels of physical and emotional discomfort and turmoil. The world is full of strife, war, riots, constant bickering. It is all humanity has ever known. Now, with seven billion people seeping through every crevice of the planet there is a tremendous amount of emotional force being produced. Open any newspaper—it is full of emotion. Now faster more efficient forms of communications serves to keep people flushed and frenzied. TV News records angry hordes surging through the streets—mass jelly like organisms bent on destruction, each a powder keg of volatile emotions. Some places on earth are little better than open sores of suffering or hives of hardship. No matter how much charity and care are thrown into the healing, the wound returns and the people continue their travail. The world has been designed to be a mesh of the harsh and the tender, the beautiful and the monstrous. Now, more than ever, the floodgates of misery are open. And we seem helpless to stop it. Medical advances are more than matched by the mounting need.

I know this is difficult to hear because it is so contrary to the sensibilities of our religion and our picture of the Divine. If you are thinking: "No, that can't be true. God loves us. God would never allow this to happen." Think about how we treat our cattle and sheep. I wonder if they could ever suspect what we are using them for? All through the Gospels Christ calls us sheep.

*

The whole universe is a big transformer broken down into many stations, like a corn stalk transforms the sun's light into energy for growth, a cow transforms grass into milk, and humans transform running water into electricity. Everything we take into our mouth gets transfigured into finer material to feed minute cells. All living things are chemical processing plants, transformers, changing the coarse into the fine. Humanity is part of an intricate system and not an end product.

Everything has its place and job in Creation. Our most critical task now is to move spiritually ahead and away from the forever grinding of the physical Universe. God is not a fairyland prince in a toy heaven, with golden streets where everybody plays the harp. God is an immense and complex enterprise, and heaven is a place of industry. We totter on the bottom rung of the ladder of life, but have been given a way to scamper up to elude the ordinary machinations of the physical world to the freedom of the spiritual world, like pure air taking flight from a dark cave.

*

This is our main chance—to work to make ourselves more worthy in spirit while all the terrestrial nonsense confronts us. We will suffer no doubt, but how we suffer tells the tale of our redemption. If we can defuse these explosives we carry around in our chest—anger, resentment, jealousy, and so on, that is the first step of an inward journey toward a gentler, genial nature that will be welcomed in the Happy Hunting Ground.

How we individually accept and deal with our troubles makes all the difference. Jesus showed us the way. After being tortured and mocked he forgave his enemies at the point of his death. He said, *"Forgive them Father for they know not what they do."*

*

One of the oldest and strangest ideas that pervade the ancient literature is that our lives are all plotted out beforehand and are watched carefully how we perform. In our reading today from the 139th Psalm, it says:

"Your eyes beheld my unformed substance. In your book were written all the days that were formed for me, when none of them as yet existed."

In many places in Shakespeare it mentions the idea of our lives being a play and we only players, but he gleaned that from much earlier writing. It was common coin among the wise. It is a key element to the esoteric teaching that is behind all religions.

The tenor and focus of our lives is set out for us. We are given exactly what we need in the way of intelligence and abilities and opportunities in order to carry out our roles. Just like members of an orchestra will tell you how they were inexorably drawn to their instrument. So it is with all of us. We are pulled to our part and fed our lines whether it is as a plumber or pianist, barrister or bartender. We have the unique tools, qualifications, and position to carry forth our duties. Our talent is the direction we go.

Our lives happen to us. It is a foolish illusion that we direct our lives. We simply ride along in them like little cars on a rail. If we can think back through our lives, we can see how circumstances were the guiding lights of our activities, not our whims. We are at the mercy of every changing event, even while presuming we are making the decisions. We take credit for something good that happened and blame ill fortune when they don't. Think about all of the things we would have liked to do, but didn't. Why didn't we? It was because we <u>couldn't</u>. The key word here is <u>couldn't</u>. Lack of Will had nothing to do with it. The oldest teaching is that we can <u>do</u> nothing. We can only <u>try</u>.

Life is not under our control, but how we process it is. If we elevate ourselves to the status of the audience, even as we act out our part, we will develop Will. Will is not doing. Will is the power of watching, an internal muscle of Attention. That is why Christ kept saying '*wake-up and watch*.'

If we ever want to change our play, we have to watch it, always be an auditor, and not be immersed in it and think it is real. Our lives are <u>not</u> real and there is nothing permanent about them—think back, even to yesterday. Doesn't it seem unreal? Almost ghost like? Nothing is the same as it was. All the people have moved. The set has changed. Yesterday's life is faded flowers.

Some people are fated for big parts on the stage, vivid lives full of tragedy and triumph. They are usually proud and boastful of their accomplishments and devastated when they end, but in fact were put into their positions by an all-powerful Necessity. Most of us are fortunate to be in the chorus away from the blinding limelight, but we are watched from above nonetheless. We are the Show and it must go on. Heavenly awards are given out for nobility of performance, not the costume. If we can remake ourselves from the inside to be able to observe ourselves before the curtain comes down, we become a star.

*

We are living on this mysterious being Nature, a sensitive film that covers the earth. But there is also a greater Being living in us, our Spirit, that someday may fly up and out and join the winged Fellowship of Heaven. It is a Fate devoutly to be wished.

When we see the picture that Jim Lovell took in 1968 of the Holy Land it should inspire us to gaze up to heaven and drop to our knees. That is how we stand highest in God's world.

Shakespeare closed out his last play with the following words. I leave them with you to ponder.

Our revels now are ended. These our actors,

215

As I foretold, you were all spirits, and
Are melted into air, into thin air.
And, like the baseless fabric of this vision,
The cloud-capped towers, the gorgeous palaces,
The solemn temples, the great globe itself—
Yea, all which it inherit – shall dissolve
And, like this insubstantial pageant faded,
Leave not a rack behind. We are such stuff
As dreams are made on, and our little life
Is rounded with a sleep.

Amen.

www.ingramcontent.com/pod-product-compliance
Lightning Source LLC
Chambersburg PA
CBHW060744050426
42449CB00008B/1301